Brink of
Destruction

BRINK OF
DESTRUCTION

A Quotable History of the
CIVIL WAR

EDITED BY
Randall Bedwell

Gramercy Books
New York

This 2002 edition is published by Gramercy Books™, an imprint of Random House Value Publishing, Inc., 280 Park Avenue, New York, NY 10017, by arrangement with Cumberland House Publishing, Inc., Nashville, Tennessee.

Gramercy Books™ and design are trademarks of Random House Value Publishing, Inc.

Some quotations have been edited for clarity and/or brevity.
All photographs courtesy of the Library of Congress.

Printed in the United States of America

Random House
New York · Toronto · London · Sydney · Auckland
http://www.randomhouse.com

A catalog record for this title is available from the Library of Congress.

ISBN: 0-517-22047-4

9 8 7 6 5 4 3 2 1

Contents

Introduction   8

1 The Coming Conflict   10
King Cotton to Lincoln's Inauguration

2 The Inescapable Conflict   30
Fort Sumter to First Manassas

3 The Brink of Destruction   56
Shiloh to Fredericksburg

4 God Bless the Cause   112
Emancipation to Vicksburg

5 We Are Going to Be Wiped Off the Earth   150
Chickamauga to Lincoln's Second Inauguration

6 We Are All Americans   190
The Road to Appomattox

7 The Border of Sorrows   206
Lincoln's Assassination and Beyond

8 A Soldier's Tale   220
Johnny Reb and Billy Yank

Brink of
Destruction

Introduction

MORE THAN a few historians have spent their professional lives researching the American Civil War and have ultimately concluded that no volume—indeed, "no series of volumes" according to one—can do justice to the critical years of 1861–65. While appreciating the wisdom in that judgment, *Brink of Destruction* hopes to accomplish its purpose by attempting less. The aim here is to extract, not to exhaust. These quotations, arranged chronologically, represent a summation of the momentous events of the war as observed and recorded by its participants. These brief utterances have been chosen for the poignancy, the insights, and in some instances, the irony implicit in the events of the war as they transpired.

A superabundance of words is an inevitable byproduct of any modern war (official communiqués, newspaper reports, war diaries, etc.); hence, a wide range of styles—from political and military rhetoric to private letters to scuttlebutt—have been included within these pages, conveying a sense of a multi-faceted, multi-voiced conversational narrative. In some instances, the spelling of the original has been maintained to preserve the genuine voice of the speaker.

Throughout, identifications of the speakers have been kept to a minimum for the sake of brevity and space. In some instances, an elaboration of circumstance or situation was deemed necessary to heighten the significance of the quotation and its inclusion. Ranks have been indicated where appropriate, and an effort has been made to confirm the rank of the individual at the time of the quotation. Thus Ulysses S. Grant is cited as brigadier general, major general, and lieutenant general. In some instances, given the recognizability of one such as Robert E. Lee, his rank has not been listed in every instance. Occasionally, a speaker's rank is unknown, and in those instances the speaker has been identified only as a Union or Confederate soldier. In most instances, soldiers have been identified by their units, such as 2d Georgia Cavalry or 54th Massachusetts Infantry, with Union or Confederate implied by the state affiliation. In ambiguous situations pertaining to the Border States of Kentucky and Missouri, Union or Confederate has been supplied.

Photographs have been included to offer depth and dimension to the citations. These have been placed to agree with the chronology of the quotations. Some have been captioned, but in several instances they appear without comment, adding their own commentary to nearby quotations.

1

The Coming Conflict

King Cotton to Lincoln's Inauguration

Well before 1832, when South Carolina first attempted to secede from the Union (a move which was quickly put down by President Andrew Jackson), Americans had begun to regard themselves as not only citizens of a new republic but also as either Northerners or Southerners. In a few short decades, the United States had become a sectionalized society whose differences drove a stubborn, immovable wedge between the two regions. "King Cotton" dominated the Southern mind, while industry fueled the North. Slavery quickly became more than just a "peculiar Southern institution." Heated congressional debate over such controversial measures as the Missouri Compromise, the Compromise of 1850, and the Fugitive Slave Law—not to mention the publication of Harriet Beecher Stowe's explosive novel, *Uncle Tom's Cabin*—brought the abhorrent practice under national scrutiny. Northern emancipators preached freedom for all, and Southern slaveowners advocated breaking all ties with the United States and forming their own country.

On October 16, 1859, radical abolitionist John Brown's attempt to incite an armed slave revolt at Harpers Ferry, Virginia, failed, giving Southern partisans such as Edmund Ruffin a very real rationalization for secession. Almost immediately, militia units formed and drilled throughout the South in anticipation of some disruption of society. More than anything else, this sense of anticipation dominated the country, predisposing Americans to act more out of fear of what might happen as opposed to what was actually happening. Warily, the slave states of the lower South expected further legislative limitations on the expansion of slavery into the new territories in the West, including possible proscriptions against slavery as it was being practiced in the

South at the time. Almost overnight the politics of compromise became the politics of confrontation.

In 1860, South Carolina's response to the election of Abraham Lincoln as president was swift and decisive. The Palmetto State seceded on December 20, thus becoming the first state to leave the Union. Mississippi, Florida, Alabama, Georgia, Louisiana, and Texas followed, and the Confederate States of America was established at a convention in Montgomery, Alabama, in February 1861.

Separation from the United States raised the question of what to do with Federal property within the seceded states. Customs houses, post offices, forts, and arsenals could only be relinquished since there was little Washington could do to prevent their confiscation. The commander of the army, Winfield Scott, pointed out to President James Buchanan that every military installation along the southern coast was undermanned and could easily be taken. Had the government wanted to garrison those forts to prevent their seizure, there were not enough troops in the army to do so. In 1860 the U.S. Army was small, spread out, and preoccupied with the western frontier.

Thus the seceded states moved to seize these properties and found little opposition. The most critical areas concerned the harbor garrisons at Charleston, South Carolina, and three Florida forts in Key West, Dry Tortugas, and Pensacola. The garrison at Charleston, however, drew the greatest scrutiny, and the relocation of Federal troops to the harbor fort known as Sumter disrupted the tenuous status quo the Buchanan administration was determined to pass on to the next administration. By the time of Lincoln's inauguration in March the stage had been set for war.

I appear this evening as a thief and robber. I stole this head, these limbs, this body from my master and ran off with them.

Frederick Douglass, from his first speech before an antislavery society, 1842

As a nation we began by declaring that all men are created equal. We now practically read it, all men are created equal except Negroes.

Abraham Lincoln, 1855

Slave-holders . . . tyrants and despots have no right to live. The only way to make the fugitive slave law a dead letter is to make half a dozen or more dead kidnappers.

Frederick Douglass, on the Fugitive Slave Law, 1856

They are beings of inferior order. So far inferior they have no rights which the white man is bound to respect.

Chief Justice Roger Taney, in the Court's majority opinion of the Dred Scott case, 1857

E nslave a man and you destroy his ambition, his enterprise, his capacity. In the constitution of human nature, the desire of bettering one's condition is the mainspring of effort.

New York Tribune *editor Horace Greeley*

In 1857 South Carolina planter James Rembert celebrated his seventy-fifth birthday by having photographs made of his family and slaves. The family was positioned at the front of the house (facing page), and the slaves were posed at the back (above).

A house divided against itself cannot stand. I believe this government cannot endure permanently, half-slave and half-free. I do not expect the Union to be dissolved—I do not expect the house to fall—but I do expect it will cease to be divided.

Abraham Lincoln, opening statement of
Lincoln-Douglas debates, June 16, 1858

No, you dare not make war on cotton. No power on earth dares to make war upon it. Cotton is king!

—Sen. John Hammond, South Carolina, 1858

I believe that to interfere, as I have done, in the behalf of God's despised poor is not wrong but right. Now, if it is deemed necessary that I should forfeit my life for the furtherance of the ends of justice, and mingle my blood further with the blood of my children and with the blood of millions in this slave country whose rights are disregarded by wicked, cruel, and unjust enactments, I say, let it be done.

John Brown, after being sentenced to death, November 1859

The murderer and robber & fire-raiser so notorious for these crimes in his Kansas career, & now the attempter of the thousand-fold horrors in Virginia, is, for these reasons, the present popular idol of the north.

Edmund Ruffin, referring to John Brown, November 27, 1859

I John Brown am now quite certain that the crimes of this guilty, land: will never be purged away; but with Blood. I had as I now think: vainly flattered myself that without much bloodshed; it might be done.

> *John Brown, December 2, 1859, the last words written from his jail cell*

This will be a great day in our history, the date of a new Revolution—quite as much needed as the old one.

> *Henry Wadsworth Longfellow, on the hanging of John Brown, December 2, 1859*

The leading northern politicians . . . do not believe that there is either courage or strength enough in the south to resist these efforts. . . . Never has there been such an opportunity for secession.

> *Edmund Ruffin, December 31, 1859*

The result proves that the plan was the attempt of a fanatic or madman.

*Lt. Col. Robert E. Lee, on John Brown's raid,
October 9, 1860*

The roaring of the approaching storm is heard from every part of the southern states.

Edmund Ruffin, November 5, 1860

I am anxious to hear from the native part of my state. I am strong for the Union at present, and if things become no worse, I hope to continue so.

*Thomas Jonathan Jackson [known
later as Stonewall Jackson], 1860*

The day of evil may never come unless we shall rashly bring it upon ourselves.

President James Buchanan, December 4, 1860

War I look for as almost certain. . . . Revolutions are much easier started than controlled, and the men who begin them [often] . . . themselves become the victims.

Alexander Stephens, early 1861

The time for compromise has now passed. The South is determined to maintain her position, and make all who oppose her smell Southern powder and feel Southern steel.

Confederate President Jefferson Davis,
February 16, 1861

For myself, I care not whether treason be committed North or South; he that is guilty of treason is entitled to a traitor's fate!

Andrew Johnson, February 1861

Let me tell you what is coming. . . . Your fathers and husbands, your sons and brothers, will be herded at the point of the bayonet. . . . You may, after the sacrifice of countless millions of treasure and of thousands of lives, as a bare possibility, win Southern independence . . . but I doubt it.

Sam Houston, governor of Texas, February 1861

South Carolina is too small for a republic and too large for an insane asylum.

> *James L. Petigru, upon hearing of the state's seceding from the Union*

Better lose a million men in battle than allow the government to be overthrown. The war will soon assume the shape of Slavery and Freedom. The world will so understand it, and I believe the final outcome will redound to the good of humanity.

> *James A. Garfield*

The shedding of blood will serve to change many . . . from the submissive or procrastinating ranks, to the zealous for immediate secession.

> *Edmund Ruffin, 1861*

Every thought that we think ought to be conciliatory, forbearing and patient.

> *William Henry Seward, Union secretary of state*

I have no purpose, directly or indirectly, to interfere with the institution of slavery in the States where it exists. I believe I have no lawful right to do so, and I have no inclination to do so.

Abraham Lincoln, First Inaugural Address, March 4, 1861

The mystic chords of memory, stretching from every battlefield and patriot grave, to every living heart and hearthstone, all over this broad land, will yet swell the chorus of the Union, when again touched, as surely they will be, by the better angels of our nature.

Abraham Lincoln, First Inaugural Address, March 4, 1861

I am with him.

Stephen A. Douglas, following Lincoln's inaugural address

If the Union is dissolved and the government disrupted, I shall return to my native state and share the miseries of my people, and save in defense, draw my sword on none.

Robert E. Lee, 1861

I have but one sentiment now: that is we have a government and laws and a flag and they must be sustained. There are but two parties now: traitors and patriots. And I want hereafter to be ranked with the latter and, I trust, the stronger party.

Ulysses S. Grant, 1861

We are divorced, North and South, because we have hated each other so.

Mary Boykin Chesnut

War means fighting, and fighting means killing.

Confederate Gen. Nathan Bedford Forrest

We will fight you to the death. Better to die a thousand deaths than to submit to live under you.

Gen. John Bell Hood

The time for war has not yet come, but it will come, and that soon; and when it does come, my advice is to draw the sword and throw away the scabbard.

Thomas Jonathan Jackson, to the cadets at the Virginia Military Institute, April 13, 1861

2

The Inescapable Conflict

Fort Sumter to First Manassas

ALTHOUGH THE South had forcibly acquired almost all federal property within its territory, the firing on Fort Sumter in Charleston Harbor on April 12, 1861, is generally looked upon as the single belligerent act that plunged the country into civil conflict. The interval between Fort Sumter and the First Battle of Manassas (or Bull Run) was filled with many bold statements about independence, honor, liberty, and duty by ardent Unionists and Confederates alike. Calls for troops were issued by both governments, and masses of recruits and a sprinkling of veterans responded and thronged the environs of Washington and the Southern capitals.

The Federal capital had few defenders in April 1861—1,000 regular army troops and 1,500 militia—and many of these were suspected of being Southern sympathizers. Virginia militia then seized the Gosport Naval Yard intact, but Fort Monroe on the Virginia Peninsula was reinforced and remained in Federal hands and controlled access to the York and James Rivers throughout the war and was also used as a staging area for the 1862 Peninsula campaign. The first Union offensive of the war, however, was to occupy the Virginia cities of Arlington and Alexandria and the area immediately across the Potomac from the Federal capital.

The recruits from the Northern states that subsequently flooded the Washington area were formed into an army of 35,000 under newly promoted Brig. Gen. Irvin McDowell. Another Union army was formed between Washington and Harpers Ferry under Maj. Gen. Robert Patterson, a veteran of the War of 1812. A third army was massing in southern Ohio under Brig. Gen. George B. McClellan. Meanwhile, more than 30,000 Southerners were converging on the

Confederate capital at Richmond, anxious to confront the Yankees and settle the war in a single battle. By July 23,000 Rebels were encamped near Manassas Junction and 10,000 occupied Harpers Ferry. At the time, few realized the long-term implications of the hasty mobilization. No general officer on either side had ever commanded such numbers of men in combat. The men themselves were untrained, undisciplined, and unprepared for battle. Nevertheless, both sides rushed into the first major battle of the war at the Manassas railway junction full of optimism, confidence, and the assurance of victory for their cause.

The battle began in the early hours of July 21, 1861, when McDowell ordered his men into action following a brief respite from the twenty-five-mile march from Washington. By midday it appeared that victory was within reach for the Northerners, but two events reversed the tide of battle: Southern cavalry under Col. J. E. B. "Jeb" Stuart disrupted the Federal advance and Rebel reinforcements arrived and were rushed to the front to buttress the Southern line. McDowell's army lost heart and fled the battlefield in a general panic.

The defeat was a crushing blow to Northern morale, but the sting of defeat steeled the Federals' resolve. Four days after the battle, McDowell was replaced, and McClellan was brought east and given the task of reorganizing and reinvigorating the Union army. Meanwhile, Southern newspapers smugly rejoiced over the victory and lionized their field commanders. Slowly, however, both sides reflected on the ferocity of the battle and realized that the end of the war would not be soon and that there would be more fighting and more losses in the future like those at Manassas.

At half-past four, the heavy booming of a cannon. I sprang out of bed. And on my knees—prostrate—I prayed as I never prayed before.

> *Mary Boykin Chesnut, on the firing of Fort Sumter, April 12, 1861*

Our Southern brethren have done grievously wrong, they have rebelled and have attacked their father's house and their loyal brothers. They must be punished and brought back, but this necessity breaks my heart.

> *Union Maj. Robert Anderson, commander of the garrison at Fort Sumter, April 14, 1861*

If it must be, let it come, and when there is no longer a soldier's arm to raise the Stars and Stripes above our Capitol, may God give me strength to mine.

> *Clara Barton, clerk in the copyright office in Washington, D.C., April 25, 1861*

A prewar view of Charleston, South Carolina (facing page), showing the Citadel in the upper foreground and the harbor in the far background.

We can only hope for peace.

Mary Todd Lincoln, April 27, 1861

My husband has wept bitter tears of blood over this terrible war, but as a man of honor and a Virginian, he must follow the destiny of his state.

Mary Custis Lee, on Robert E. Lee's resignation from the Union army, April 21, 1861

We feel that our cause is just and holy. . . . In independence we seek no conquest, no aggrandizement, no cession of any kind from the States with which we have lately confederated. All we ask is to be let alone.

Confederate President Jefferson Davis, April 29, 1861

Maj. Robert Anderson and the officers under his command at Fort Sumter posed for Charleston photographer George Cook in February 1861. They are (front row, left to right) Abner Doubleday, Anderson, Samuel W. Crawford, John G. Foster, (standing, left to right) Truman Seymour, George W. Snyder, Jefferson C. Davis, Richard K. Meade, and Theodore Talbot. All but Meade, Snyder, and Talbot would be generals by the end of the war, and one of these, Meade, resigned from the army after the fall of Sumter to fight for the South.

There are only two sides to the question. Every man must be for the United States or against it. There can be no neutrals in this war, only patriots—or traitors.

Sen. Stephen A. Douglas, April 1861

I hope God is on our side, but I've got to have Kentucky.

Abraham Lincoln, emphasizing the critical importance of the Border States in the conflict, April 1861

If we are fighting for the annihilation of slavery, to be sure, it may be a wise object, and offer a tangible result, and the only one which is consistent with a future reunion between North and South.

Nathaniel Hawthorne, May 1861

They do not know what they say. If it comes to a conflict of arms, the war will last at least four years. Northern politicians do not appreciate the determination and pluck of the South, and Southern politicians do not appreciate the numbers, resources, and patient perseverance of the North. Both sides forget that we are all Americans. I foresee that the country will have to pass through a terrible ordeal, a necessary expiation, perhaps, for our national sins.

Confederate Gen. Robert E. Lee, May 5, 1861

I think it is to be a long war—very long—much longer than any politician thinks.

Union Col. William Tecumseh Sherman, June 3, 1861

Militia units responded from throughout the South to occupy and garrison Federal sites within the seceded states. Even after the call for men to defend the Confederate capital at Richmond, to which these units responded with eager thoughts of glory and victory, the men were occupied with more mundane tasks, such as drilling and even construction work since most of the fortifications were in need of repair, not from battle, but from neglect. This South Carolina unit was photographed at Castle Pinckney in Charleston Harbor in August 1861.

To hear the young orators tell of how they would protect the flag, and that they would come back with the flag or come back not at all, and if they fell they would fall with their backs to the field and their feet to the foe, would fairly make our hair stand on end with intense patriotism, and we wanted to march right off and whip twenty Yankees.

> *Confederate Pvt. Sam Watkins, 1st Tennessee Infantry, following a flag presentation ceremony to his regiment*

Mind what I tell you: You fellows will catch the devil before you get through with this business.

> *Union Adm. David Glasgow Farragut, to seceding Southerners*

We seceded to rid ourselves of the rule of the majority.

> *Jefferson Davis*

The central idea of secession is the essence of anarchy.

Abraham Lincoln

To fight against slaveholders, without fighting against slavery, is but a half-hearted business. . . . Fire must be met with water. . . . War for the destruction of liberty must be met with war for the destruction of slavery.

Frederick Douglass, 1861

I express it as my conviction before God that it is the duty of every American citizen to rally round the flag of his country.

Sen. Stephen A. Douglas, 1861

Ours is not a revolution. We are not engaged in a Quixotic fight for the rights of man; our struggle is for inherited rights.

Jefferson Davis, 1861

This is essentially a People's contest. On the side
of the Union, it is a struggle for maintaining in the
world, that form, and substance of government,
whose leading object is, to elevate the condition of
men—to lift artificial weights from all shoulders—
to clear the paths of laudable pursuit for all—to
afford all, an unfettered start, and a fair chance,
in the race of life.

Abraham Lincoln, July 4, 1861

Everything seems to be in "status quo." Each party
is awaiting for the other to make the attack.

Capt. Thomas J. Goree, Longstreet's staff

We looked forward to the time when we could
give the Yankees a taste of our steel, and we
were confident that when the time came we would
be victorious.

Pvt. Robert S. Hudgins, 3d Virginia Cavalry

The whole campaign has been a grand mistake, bad in its inception, bad in its conduct, really only good in the retreat from a position unfortunately taken.

> *Col. William B. Taliaferro, 23d Virginia Infantry,*
> *following the battle of Rich Mountain in*
> *western Virginia*

Colonel [Israel] Richardson's remarks to the Major, when he discovered our position, and proceeded to unravel us, were not of a character to be repeated, even at this late date.

> *Asst. Surgeon Henry F. Lyster, 2d Michigan Infantry,*
> *at Blackburn's Ford*

I heard occasional dropping shots in the camp. To my looks of inquiry, an engineer said quietly: "They are volunteers shooting themselves." The number of accidents and the carelessness of the men is astonishing. In every day's paper, there is a count of deaths and wounded caused by the discharge of firearms in the tents.

> London Times *correspondent William Howard Russell,*
> *July 1861*

Y ou are green, it is true, but they are green, also;
you are all green alike.

> *Abraham Lincoln, to Gen. Irvin McDowell before the*
> *battle of First Manassas*

I went to the tent of Genl. McDowell and had quite a
conversation with him. I never had much of an
opinion of him as a General, and I left his tent with a
feeling of great sadness and a sort of prescience of
coming disaster.

> *Elihu B. Washburne, congressman from Illinois*

L et tomorrow be their Waterloo.

> *Confederate Gen. Pierre Gustave Toutant Beauregard,*
> *July 19, 1861*

M en fall. They are bleeding, torn and mangled. The
trees are splintered as if smitten by thunderbolts. There
is smoke, dust, wild talking, shouting, hissings,
howlings, explosions. It's a strange, new, unanticipated
experience to the soldiers of both armies.

> Boston Journal *reporter Charles C. Coffin, July 1861*

I cannot give you an idea of the terrors of this battle. For ten long hours, it literally rained balls, shells, and other missiles of destruction. The sight of the dead, the cries of the wounded, the thundering noise of battle can never be put on paper. The dead, the dying, and the wounded all mixed up together. Friend and foe embraced in death. Some crying for water. Some praying their last prayers. Some trying to whisper to a friend their last farewell message to their loved ones at home. It was heartrendering.

Confederate soldier Jesse Reed,
8th South Carolina Infantry

I have been under many a hot fire, but I don't think that, in nearly four years experience, I ever heard so many bullets in such a short space of time [as I did at First Manassas].

Lt. J. Albert Monroe, Rhode Island Artillery

The two armies mauled each other throughout the day of July 21, 1861, and the Union would have carried the day had it not been for Stuart's cavalry and the timely arrival of reinforcements from western Virginia. After the battle of Manassas, both sides saw what neither had imagined possible: 900 dead and more than 3,000 wounded and missing. This war was to be fought at an infinitely more destructive level than anyone had expected. What Americans failed to comprehend was that the battles that were to follow would be even larger and deadlier. Shiloh would have 23,000 casualties, and Gettysburg would have more than 50,000.

We were exposed to the concentrated fire of the entire rebel force then in action, and the sounds of their missiles, running through the whole scale of warlike music, from the savage rush of twelve pound shells to the spiteful "pish" of the minie bullets, was ruinous to weak nerves.

Pvt. Martin A. Haynes, 2d New Hampshire Infantry

When we got to Bull Run at Sudley's Ford, many stopped to drink; scooped up muddy water in their hands, their hats, their shoes; drank too much; were lost to service for that day. Not half the brigade, nor half the regiment, crossed the run.

Sgt. Abner R. Small, 3d Maine Infantry

I looked around and I was all alone.

Pvt. George S. Barnsley, 8th Georgia Infantry

Gentlemen, you have got me, but a hundred thousand more await you.

Confederate prisoner

Look, men! There stands Jackson like a stone wall. Rally behind the Virginians!

> *Confederate Gen. Barnard E. Bee,*
> *during the battle of First Manassas*

[General Jackson] had his hand raised, wrapped in a handkerchief, and was evidently wounded, but he refused to dodge. I do not know whether I tried to imitate him or not, but I dare say I bowed involuntarily more than one.

> *Pvt. Clement D. Fishburne, Rockbridge Artillery*

The instant the [Stars and Stripes] appeared, Stuart ordered the charge, and at them we went like an arrow from a bow.

> *Lt. William W. Blackford, 1st Virginia Cavalry*

The enemy had now approached within a hundred yards and poured a volley into this howling mob; it was then "Skiddo," every man for himself and the devil take the hindmost.

> *1st Sgt. Josias R. King, 1st Minnesota Infantry*

How I got off the field I am at loss to tell; but I did get away and made for the woods.

Pvt. Harrison H. Comings, 11th New York Infantry

It's a d— disagreeable thing to be whipped.

Col. William Tecumseh Sherman,
Union brigade commander

Just then—can I ever forget it?—there came, as it seemed, an instantaneous suppression of firing, and almost immediately a cheer went up and ran along the valley from end to end of our line. It meant victory.

Pvt. George W. Bagby, clerk on Beauregard's staff

I went to and fro obtaining the names of killed, wounded, and missing. These I scrawled upon bits of newspaper, upon envelopes, upon the lining of my hat, and finally upon my shirt wristbands. I was literally filled with notes, and if I had been shot, endeavors to obtain my name would have been extremely difficult.

New York Herald *reporter George Alfred Townsend*

Defeat was not the most unpleasant fate for many Union troops at Manassas; these men of the New York Fire Zouaves (facing page) were captured and imprisoned in Charleston Harbor at Castle Pinckney, awaiting exchange.

No curse could be greater than invasion by a volunteer army. McDowell and all of the generals tried their best. But to say he commanded that army is no such thing. They did as they pleased.

Col. William Tecumseh Sherman,
Union brigade commander

Defeat was the best thing that could have happened to us; for it humbled us and made us make better preparations which led in time to a final victory.

Col. Oliver O. Howard, Union brigade commander

If the Rebels are not to be beaten, then every drop of blood henceforth shed in this quarrel will be wantonly, wickedly shed. It is best for the country and for mankind that we make peace with the Rebels at once, and on their own terms. Do not shrink even from that.

New York Tribune *editor Horace Greeley, July 1861*

Whilst great credit is due to other parts of our gallant army, God made my brigade more instrumental than any other.

> *Gen. Thomas Jonathan "Stonewall" Jackson*
> *after First Manassas*

Today will be known as BLACK MONDAY. We are utterly and disgracefully routed, beaten, whipped by secessionists.

> *George Templeton Strong, after First Manassas,*
> *July 22, 1861*

I cannot express the joy I feel at the brilliant victory of the 21st. . . . You and your troops have the gratitude of the whole country.

> *Confederate Gen. Robert E. Lee to General Beauregard*
> *following the battle of First Manassas*

It is not characteristic of Americans to sit down despondently after a defeat. . . . Reverses, though stunning at first, by their recoil stimulate and quicken to unwonted exertion. . . . Let us go to work, then, with a will.

New York Tribune, *July 30, 1861*

The president is an idiot! I only wish to save my country and find the incapables around me will not permit it.

Union Gen. George B. McClellan, August 1861

Whenever you see anything blue, shoot at it, and do all you can to keep up the scare.

Confederate Gen. Nathan Bedford Forrest

The South was confident of success in its war for independence after the battle of Manassas, and that pluck and pride carried its armies through incredible hardships over the
next four years. The Home Guard battery above, photographed in 1863, hints at that
spirit as this group of Charlestonians, some of whom are boys, mans its guns at Fort
Pemberton, overlooking the Stono River. The effectiveness of this and other batteries on
James Island contributed to Southern success at the battle of Secessionville in June 1862
and blunted any further Federal attempts toward the overland conquest of Charleston.

3

The Brink of Destruction

Shiloh to Fredericksburg

FOLLOWING THE battle of First Bull Run, both sides prepared for a long, protracted struggle. With the fall of Forts Henry and Donelson (situated on the Cumberland River) in February 1862 and the evacuation of Nashville by Confederate forces, the North scored its first victories, striking deep into the heartland of the Confederacy. Gen. Ulysses S. Grant gained a national reputation when his famous ultimatum demanding unconditional surrender became widely circulated.

Grant also figured prominently in the Union's next great success in the West. Many soldiers experienced their first taste of combat near a lonely little church house in southern Tennessee called Shiloh, not far from the Tennessee River. On the first day of fighting on April 6, 1862, the Rebels seized the element of surprise and the initial momentum with an early morning attack. During the afternoon, however, the Federal line stiffened, and Confederate Gen. Albert Sidney Johnston—overall Southern military commander in the western theater and the South's ablest soldier in the opinion of many—was mortally wounded astride his mount. Responsibility for the assault devolved upon Gen. P. G. T. Beauregard, the hero of Fort Sumter and the battle of First Manassas, who called off the effort as nightfall approached and anticipated victory the next day. Federal reinforcements, however, arrived from Nashville and were ferried across the river overnight, fueling a Union counterattack the following day that drove the Rebels back to Corinth, Mississippi.

On the Virginia front, the North's situation was not as encouraging. In Washington, D.C., Lincoln gave overall command of Union forces to Gen. George B. McClellan, who had made a name for himself with several successes in western Virginia. The new commander's first task was to organize the mass of Federal volunteers into an army, but once that was accomplished McClellan seemed hesitant to engage the Confederates. When pressed on the issue, he unveiled a bold offensive that called for the amphibious mobilization of his army from the outskirts of the capital to the Virginia Peninsula leading into Richmond, the Confederate capital. After a promising start, McClellan's Army of the Potomac almost met with disaster on the peninsula, facing first Joseph E. Johnston and then Robert E. Lee. With the spires of Richmond's churches in sight, the Yankee army fell back in the face of a sudden Confederate offensive known as the Seven Days' battles. Almost immediately the tide of the war had turned in favor of the Confederacy.

As McClellan's army withdrew from the peninsula, another Union army, commanded by John Pope, invaded Virginia and collided with forces coordinated by Lee near the old Manassas battlefield. Lee's army crushed Pope's.

Following that victory and with no Union army on Virginia soil, Lee boldly initiated an invasion of the North. When the Army of Northern Virginia marched into Maryland, the command structure of the Union army was in shambles. With no one else to turn to and panic setting in around Washington with news of Lee's movements, Lincoln again gave command of the Federal army to McClellan.

The two armies came together near the town of Sharpsburg. On September 17, 1862, the Southerners stood off three uncoordinated Northern assaults, but neither army could resume the fight the next day. That evening Lee's army withdrew across the Potomac and back into Virginia. McClellan claimed victory, but he failed to exploit the opportunity to pursue Lee's weakened army. The empty Union victory at Antietam prompted Lincoln to issue the Emancipation Proclamation five days later, thus putting the North's fight squarely on the side of human rights and against slavery.

With consistent Confederate victories in the East and a stalled Union advance in the West, Lincoln's Emancipation Proclamation was perceived by most Southerners as an empty gesture. Indeed, some planters did not learn of the executive order freeing their slaves until the slaves themselves—many of whom fled servitude for the haven of Union lines—told them! Although the proclamation had little immediate effect legally, it promised eventual freedom to the most repressed element in Southern society and gave the North a much-needed edge in the war for world opinion.

Nevertheless, the Union effort was in chaos. Lincoln relieved McClellan of command, reassigned Pope to defend the Minnesota frontier, and promoted wary Ambrose E. Burnside to command the Army of the Potomac. By then, Lee's forces were spread across northern Virginia, and Burnside saw an opportunity to advance on Richmond by moving his army to Fredericksburg, crossing the Rappahannock River, and approaching Richmond from the south. Had his efforts been coordinated better, he might have succeeded. Instead, Federal supplies were slow in reaching him, which allowed Lee time to reform his army *en mass* on the heights above Fredericksburg.

In the time allowed by Burnside's delays, the Southerners entrenched behind perhaps the greatest defensive fortifications of the war. Sharpshooters were dispatched to the town to harass the efforts of the Federals to cross the Rappahannock. When they proved highly effective, Yankee artillery opened on the town, but the shelling failed to repel the sharpshooters. Finally, three Northern regiments crossed the river by boat and engaged in house-to-house fighting to dislodge the Confederate riflemen.

When Burnside's army assembled in Fredericksburg, it found itself at the mercy of Lee's artillery and several regiments stationed behind a stone wall near the crest of a hilly slope. Here Burnside's offensive was blunted on December 13, and the Union force suffered incredible losses before pulling back. Burnside tried to refit his army and renew his offensive, but Lincoln removed him from command, and the army returned to its Washington camps to await the spring.

Tears may be ours, but proud, for those who win
Death's royal purple in the foeman's lines;
Peace, too, brings tears; and mid the battle-din,
The wiser ear some text of God divines,
For the sheathed blade may rust with darker sin.

James Russell Lowell, poet, from "The Washers of the Shroud," October 1861

Our people have thought too much of themselves and their ease, and instead of turning out to a man, have been content to nurse themselves and their dimes, and leave the protection of themselves and families to others. . . . This is not the way to accomplish our independence.

Confederate Gen. Robert E. Lee, 1861

Before this war is over, I intend to be a major general or a corpse.

Confederate Gen. Isaac Trimble

Abolition is not to be the object of the war, but simply one of its agencies.

> *Sen. Charles Sumner, Massachusetts, November 1861*

Free every slave—slay every traitor—burn every Rebel mansion, if these things be necessary to preserve this temple of freedom.

> *Congressman Thaddeus Stevens, Pennsylvania, 1861*

Takeing the whole thing into Consideration it was one of the Completest victorys that has yet been achieved.

> *Pvt. Thomas F. Miller, 29th Illinois Infantry, at Fort Henry, Tennessee*

It was, perhaps, in the ordination of Providence that we were taught the value of our liberties by the price we pay for them.

> *Jefferson Davis, after the Confederate defeat at Fort Donelson, February 1862*

Far better that this grinding should go on, bad and worse, than we should be driven by any impatience into a hasty peace restoring the old rottenness.

Ralph Waldo Emerson, January 1, 1862

No terms except unconditional and immediate surrender can be accepted.

Union Gen. Ulysses S. Grant, at Fort Donelson, Tennessee, February 16, 1862

The first time I ever saw General [Nathan Bedford] Forrest was in the gray dawn of the morning of the surrender [of Fort Donelson]. . . . He saw I was mounted, and called to me and asked if I did not want to go out with him. I told him I did not think I ought to leave my command, but ought to share their fate. He turned with the remark: "All right; I admire your loyalty, but d— your judgment."

Pvt. John S. Wilkes, 3d Tennessee Infantry

The rebels evacuated Bowling and Nashville like a flock of sheep chased with dogs. They burn bridges and destroy property and then run like the devil.

Sgt. Michael S. Bright, 77th Pennsylvania Infantry

The destiny of the colored American . . . is the destiny of America.

Frederick Douglass, 1862

A thoughtful mind, when it sees a nation's flag, sees not the flag only, but the nation itself; and whatever may be its symbols, its insignia, be read chiefly in the flag of the government, the principles, the truths, the history which belongs to the nation that sets it forth.

Henry Ward Beecher, "The National Flag," 1861

Conquer or be conquered.

Union Adm. David Farragut

The character of the war has very much changed within the last year. There can be no peace but that which is enforced with the sword. We must conquer the rebels, or be conquered by them. This is the phase which the rebellion has now assumed.

Union Gen. Henry W. Halleck, March 20, 1862

I hoped and expected that I had others who would prove generals, but I knew I had one, and that was [Albert] Sidney Johnston.

Jefferson Davis, September 1861

The roads will be ready to move over in a few days and then God keep the Rebel soldiers for the Lincolnites will not.

Pvt. George S. Richardson, 6th Iowa Infantry

The main force of the enemy is at Corinth. I have scarcely the faintest idea of an attack being made upon us.

Brig. Gen. Ulysses S. Grant

We must do something or die in the attempt. Otherwise, all will be shortly lost.

> *Confederate Gen. Pierre Gustave Toutant Beauregard, Shiloh, April 1862*

We did not fortify our camps against attack, because we had no orders to do so, and because such a course would have made our raw men timid.

> *Brig. Gen. William Tecumseh Sherman*

I marvelled, as I heard the unintermitting patter, snip, thud, and hum of the bullets, how anyone could live under this raining death.

> *Pvt. Henry M. Stanley, 6th Arkansas Infantry*

Boys, don't be discouraged; that is not the first charge that was ever repulsed; fix bayonets and give them steel.

> *Confederate Brig. Gen. Patrick R. Cleburne*

Someone recently mentioned the wonderful resources of old Tennessee, . . . but a fine young oak at Shiloh . . . was the most valuable piece I ever saw.

Pvt. M. E. Boysell, 58th Ohio Infantry

I thought it strange that a Sunday should have been chosen to disturb the holy calm of those woods.

Pvt. Henry W. Stanley, 6th Arkansas Infantry

Retreat? No. I propose to attack at daylight and whip them.

Union Gen. Ulysses S. Grant to Col. James McPherson, Shiloh, April 6, 1862

We'll be whipped like hell tomorrow.

Confederate Gen. Nathan Bedford Forrest, prior to the Union's victorious counterattack on the second day of battle at Shiloh, April 6, 1862

The scenes on this field would have cured anybody of war.

Union Gen. William Tecumseh Sherman

If defeated here, we lose . . . our cause.

Confederate Gen. Pierre Gustave Toutant Beauregard, Corinth, Mississippi, 1862

Action, action is what we want and what we must have.

Union Gen. George B. McClellan, 1862

If this Valley [the Shenandoah] is lost, Virginia is lost.

Confederate Gen. T. J. "Stonewall" Jackson

Of the civil war I say only this. It is Slavery against Freedom; the north wind against the southern pestilence.

Henry Wadsworth Longfellow, May 8, 1862

Mother, Home, Heaven are all sweet words, but the grandest sentence I ever heard from mortal lips was uttered this evening by Captain [R. Preston] Chew when he said, "Boys, the battle is over."

Cpl. George M. Neese, Chew's Virginia Battery

George B. McClellan (facing page, to the right of the stump) was photographed at Upton Hill, Virginia, during the Peninsula campaign.

It seems as if we had no plan and no courage
or decision. Vacillation is our name. We cannot
take Jackson.

Lt. Col. Wilder Dwight, 2d Massachusetts Infantry

Every man seemed to think he was on a chessboard
and Jackson played us to suit his purpose. The enemy
was in the dark as much as we were.

Sgt. Samuel D. Buck, 13th Virginia Infantry

Our men curse [Jackson] for the hard marching he
makes them do, but still the privates of the whole
army have the most unbounded confidence in him.
They say he can take them into harder places and get
them out better than any other living man.

Col. Samuel Fulkerson, 37th Virginia Infantry

I intend to be careful. Don't let them [Congress]
hurry me, is all I ask.

Union Gen. George B. McClellan

War is a game of chance, and besides the chances of service, the accidents and luck of the field, in our army, an officer has to run the chances of having his political friends in power, or able to work for him.

Union Gen. George Gordon Meade, May 10, 1862

I have just heard one of my brothers was killed in the war. Since he chose to be our deadly enemy, I see no reason why I should bitterly mourn his death. Why should I sympathize with the Rebels? They would hang my husband tomorrow if it was in their power.

Mary Todd Lincoln, 1862

By some strange operation of magic I have become the power of the land. . . . God has placed a great work in my hands. . . . I was called to do it; my previous life seems to have been unwittingly directed to this great end.

Union Gen. George B. McClellan, 1862

The best remembered military event of the winter of 1861–2 was the grand review at Bailey's Crossroads. . . . [T]he ground trembled under the steady tread of the endless columns of disciplined soldiers and the air throbbed with the music of countless bands, the all pervading feeling was an enthusiastic and ardent admiration for the man who had created the Army of the Potomac.

Col. William W. Averell, 3d Pennsylvania Cavalry

A battery of field artillery is worth a thousand muskets.

Union Gen. William Tecumseh Sherman

It seems clear that I shall have the whole forces of the enemy on my hands, probably not less than 100,000 men, and possibly more.

Union Gen. George B. McClellan, April 7, 1862

I regard it as certain that the enemy will meet us with all his force on or near the Chickahominy. . . . If I am not re-enforced, it is probable that I will be obliged to fight nearly double my numbers, strongly intrenched.

Union Gen. George B. McClellan, May 10, 1862

I feel sure of success, so good is the spirit of my men and so great their ardor. But I am tired of the battlefield, with its mangled corpses and poor wounded. Victory has no charms for me when purchased at such a cost.

Union Gen. George B. McClellan, June 2, 1862

If there is one man in either army, Confederate or Federal, head and shoulders above any other in audacity, it is General Lee! His name might be Audacity. He will take more desperate chances, and take them quicker, than any other general in this country, North or South.

Confederate Col. Joseph Ives

The shot that struck me down is the very best that has been fired for the Southern cause yet. While [I possess] no degree the confidence of the government, now they have in my place one who does possess it.

Confederate Gen. Joseph E. Johnston, commenting on the promotion of Lee to command the Southern army, June 1862

I prefer Lee to Johnston. The former is too cautious and weak under grave responsibility—personally brave and energetic to a fault, he yet is wanting in moral firmness when pressed by heavy responsibility and is likely to be timid and irresolute in action.

Union Gen. George B. McClellan

At a yard near Savage Station, Virginia, these men from the 16th New York Infantry were taken prisoner following the battle of Gaines's Mill. The New Yorkers wore straw hats during the June battle, a gift from the wife of one of the officers who thought the headwear would be appropriate for the weather. The hats, however, made good targets, and the unit allegedly suffered a high number of head injuries during the fighting

Can anyone say they know Robert E. Lee?

Mary Boykin Chesnut

McClellan will make this a battle of posts. He will take position from position, under cover of his heavy guns. I am preparing a line that I can hold with part of our forces in front, while the rest I will endeavor to make a diversion to bring McClellan out.

Robert E. Lee, June 1862

If I save the army now, I tell you plainly that I owe no thanks to you or any other persons in Washington.

Union Gen. George B. McClellan, to Secretary of War
Edwin M. Stanton, June 28, 1862

As I stood [on Malvern Hill] just a little after sunrise and looked for the first time upon our whole or very nearly our whole army I could hardly conceive any power that could overwhelm us.

Capt. Edward A. Acton, 5th New Jersey Infantry,
July 1, 1862

With jackets off and shirt sleeves rolled up, with faces wet with perspiration and begrimed with the smoke, in the light of the sudden flash from their guns [the Union gunners] looked as much like devils as men.

Sgt. Frederick E. Garnett, 74th New York Infantry

As each brigade emerged from the woods, from fifty to one hundred guns opened upon it, tearing great gaps in its ranks. But the heroes reeled on and were shot down by the reserves of the guns. Most of them had an open field half a mile wide to cross under fire of field artillery. It was not war, it was murder.

Confederate Gen. Daniel Harvey Hill, Malvern Hil

The idea of stealing away in the night from such a position, after such a victory, was simply galling.

Capt. William Biddle, aide on McClellan's staff

Under normal circumstances the Federal Army should have been destroyed.

Robert E. Lee

War is horrible because it strangles youth.
Union Gen. Philip Kearny, June 1862

Generals must observe discipline as well as private soldiers.

Union Gen. George B. McClellan, 1862

I expect to maintain this contest until successful, or till I die, or am conquered, or my term expires, or Congress or the country forsakes me.

Abraham Lincoln, June 28, 1862

I have come to you from the West, where we have always seen the backs of our enemies; from an army whose business it has been to seek the adversary and to beat him when he was found; whose policy has been attack and not defense.

Union Gen. John Pope

I want Pope suppressed.

Robert E. Lee

[J]ackson's] face was lit with the inspiration of heroism. The men would have followed him into the jaws of death itself; nothing could have stopped them and nothing did.

Capt. Charles M. Blackford, 2d Virginia Cavalry

This war was undertaken by us to shake off the yoke of foreign invaders, so we consider our cause righteous. The Yankees, since the war has begun, have discovered it is to free the slaves that they are fighting, so their cause is noble.

Mary Boykin Chesnut, July 8, 1862

We must free the slaves or be ourselves subdued . . . and strike at the heart of the rebellion.

Abraham Lincoln, July 13, 1862

Slavery will be sent out by this agony. We are only in the throes and ravings of the exorcism. The roots of the cancer have gone everywhere, but they must die—and will.

Harriet Beecher Stowe, author of Uncle Tom's Cabin, *July 31, 1862*

The very stomach of this rebellion is the negro in the form of a slave. Arrest that hoe in the hands of a negro, and you smite the rebellion in the very seat of its life.

Frederick Douglass

I will hold McClellan's horse if he will only bring us success.

Abraham Lincoln, 1862

One flag, one land, one heart, one hand
One Nation, evermore!

Oliver Wendell Holmes, 1862

Before any orders could be given to change position, the balls began to fly from the woods like hail. It was a continual hiss, snap, whizz & slug.

> *Pvt. Alfred Davenport, 5th New York Infantry,*
> *at Second Manassas*

War has been designated as Hell, and I can assure you than where the Regiment stood that day was the very vortex of Hell. Not only were men wounded, or killed, but they were riddled.

> *Pvt. Andrew Coats, 5th New York Infantry*

An acre of ground was literally covered with the dead, dying, and wounded of the Fifth New York Zouaves, the variegated colors of whose peculiar uniform gave the scene the appearance of a Texas hillside in spring, painted with wild flowers of every hue and color.

> *Cpl. Joseph B. Polley, 4th Texas Infantry*

Before I die let me implore that in some way it may be stated that General Pope has been outwitted, and that [Irvin] McDowell is a traitor.

Col. Thornton F. Brodhead, 1st Michigan Cavalry

Well, we are whipped again, I am afraid. What shall we do? The bottom is out of the tub, the bottom is out of the tub!

Abraham Lincoln, responding to the Union debacle at Second Manassas, August 1862

Battle after battle—disaster after disaster. . . . The power they are bringing to bear against our country is tremendous. . . . The reality is hideous.

Mary Boykin Chesnut, 1862

My paramount object in this struggle is to save the Union, and is not either to save or to destroy slavery. If I could save the Union without freeing any slave I would do it, and if I could save it by freeing all the slaves I would do it; and if I could save it by freeing some and leaving others alone I would also do that.

Abraham Lincoln, August 22, 1862, in an open letter to New York Tribune *editor Horace Greeley*

Always mystify, mislead, and surprise the enemy; and when you strike and overcome him, never let up in the pursuit. Never fight against heavy odds if you can hurl your own force on only a part of your enemy and crush it. A small army may thus destroy a large one and repeated victory will make you invincible.

Confederate Gen. Thomas J. "Stonewall" Jackson

Whatever Lee's plans are, they will be good, and his army can carry them out.

Confederate Lt. John H. Chamberlayne

We must use the tools we have. There is no man in the army who can man these fortifications and lick these troops of ours into shape half as well as he. If he can't fight himself, he excels in making others ready to fight.

Abraham Lincoln, explaining his decision to restore McClellan to command the Army of the Potomac, September 5, 1862

I could see dimly through the dense sulphurous battle smoke and the line from Shakespeare's Tempest flitted across my brain: Hell is empty and all the devils are here.

Pvt. Frederick C. Foard, 20th North Carolina Infantry, battle of South Mountain

I saw him sitting there gently reclined against the tree, essentially old, this boy of scarcely sixteen summers. His cap had fallen to the ground on one side, his hand resting on his knee. It clasped a little testament opened at some familiar place. He wore the gray. He was my enemy, this boy. He was dead—the boy, my enemy—but I shall see him forever.

Union Maj. Joshua Lawrence Chamberlain, September 17, 1862, at South Mountain en route to Antietam

The brave Union commander, superbly mounted, placed himself in front, while his band cheered them with martial music. I thought, "What a pity to spoil with bullets such a scene of martial beauty."

Col. John B. Gordon, 6th Alabama Infantry

There was, on the part of the men, great hysterical excitement, eagerness to go forward, and a reckless disregard of life, of everything but victory.

Maj. Rufus Dawes, 6th Wisconsin Infantry

The smoke coming from the artillery hung heavily over the fields, and as the sunlight pierced it, the grayish tints disappeared, and there was left a blue sulphurous tinge, the incarnate color of battle.

Pvt. William F. Goodhue, 3d Wisconsin Infantry

There is nothing on this green earth half so grand as the sight of soldiers moving into action. A cavalry charge is superb; artillery dashing on the field carries you away; while the deadly infantry moving into the jaws of death causes you to hold your breath in admiration.

Sgt. William H. Andrews, 1st Georgia Infantry

We were upon a field where more glory was to be achieved, more colors to be captured, more guns taken or silenced, more of the enemy to be placed *hors de combat*, and more of our men to demonstrate their love for their country by the shedding of their life's blood.

Pvt. Joseph L. Cornet, 28th Pennsylvania Infantry

Those of us who were yet living got back to the edge of the cornfield, and opened such a fire, that, though the enemy charged five times to gain possession of the flag, they were driven back each time with terrible slaughter.

Lt. Charles B. Tanner, 1st Delaware Infantry

The last scene on which my eye rested that night before it closed . . . was that of a small group with a flickering lantern beside a fence near by, who were digging a grave and rudely raising the earth over some fellow-soldier who had fallen.

Sgt. George W. Beale, 9th Virginia Cavalry

Instead of a decided brilliant victory and the end of the war, we have a doubtful victory and the enemy left to recruit at will and prolong the contest indefinitely.

Surgeon Daniel M. Holt, 121st New York Infantry

It was a dreadful scene. The dead and dying lay thick on the field like harvest sheaths. The pitiable cries for water and pleas for help were much more horrible to listen to than the deadliest sounds of battle. Silent were the dead and motionless, but here and there were raised stiff arms. Heads made a last effort to raise themselves from the ground. Prayers were mingled with oaths, and midnight hid all distinction between blue and gray.

Henry Kyd Douglas, aide on Jackson's staff, September 17, 1862

I hope that I may never see such a sight again. The dead were thicker here than I had seen them anywhere else.

Union Lt. Tully McCrea, following the battle of Antietam, September 1862

The spectacle yesterday was the grandest I could conceive of. Nothing could be more sublime. Those on whose judgement I rely tell me that I fought the battle splendidly, and that it was a masterpiece of art.

Union Gen. George B. McClellan, September 18, 1862

The fiery trial through which we pass, will light us down, in honor or dishonor, to the last generation. . . . The dogmas of the quiet past are inadequate to the stormy present. . . . In giving freedom to the slave, we assure freedom to the free. . . . We must disenthral ourselves, and then we shall save our country.

Abraham Lincoln, September 22, 1862

Every stalk of corn in the northern and greater part of the field was cut as closely as could have been done with a knife, and the slain lay in rows precisely as they had stood in their ranks a few moments before. It was never my fortune to witness a more bloody, dismal battlefield.

Union Gen. Joseph Hooker, report on the fighting at Antietam, November 8, 1862

On the first day of January in the year of Our Lord one thousand eight hundred and sixty-three, all persons held as slaves within any state or a designated part of a state, the people whereof shall then be in rebellion against the United States, shall be then thence forward and forever free.

The Emancipation Proclamation

In giving freedom to the slave, we assure freedom to the free. We shall nobly save or meanly lose the last best hope of earth.

Abraham Lincoln, describing the
Emancipation Proclamation, September 1862

We shout for joy that we live to record this righteous decree.

Frederick Douglass, after hearing the announcement of
the Emancipation Proclamation, September 22, 1862

If we never try, we shall never succeed.

> *Abraham Lincoln, October 1862*

In my feeble estimation, General McClellan, with all his laurels, sinks into insignificance beside the true heroine of the age, the angel of the battlefield.

> *Dr. James Dunn, referring to Clara Barton in a letter to his wife after the battle of Antietam*

Dulce et decorum est pro patria mori. (It is sweet and fitting to die for one's country.)

> *Motto of Union Gen. Philip Kearny, killed September 1, 1862, at Chantilly, Virginia*

The dead of the battle-field come up to us very rarely, even in dreams. We see the list in the morning paper at breakfast, but dismiss its recollection with coffee. . . . It is like a funeral next door. It attracts your attention but does not enlist your sympathy. But it is very different when the hearse stops at your own door and the corpse is carried out over your own threshold. Those who lose friends in battle know what battlefields are. . . . Mr. Brady has done something to bring home to us the terrible reality and earnestness of war. If he has not brought bodies and laid them in our door-yards and along the streets, he has done something very like it. . . . These pictures have a terrible distinctiveness.

> New York Times, *in a review of an exhibit at Mathew Brady's salon of photographs taken on the Antietam battlefield by Alexander Gardner, October 1862*

When Lincoln relieved McClellan of command for a second time, Maj. Gen. Joseph Hooker (above left) vied for the appointment. The president, however, had reservations about Hooker and gave command to Ambrose E. Burnside (above right) despite Burnside's protestations.

The picturesque town of Fredericksburg (facing page) was halfway between Washington and Richmond on the main road connecting the two cities and was connected to the Confederate capital by railroad and by river.

Oh, I know where Lee's forces are, and I expect to surprise him. I expect to cross [the Rappahannock] and occupy the hills before Lee can bring anything serious against me.

Union Gen. Ambrose E. Burnside

101

If you make the attack as contemplated, it will be the greatest slaughter of the war; there isn't infantry enough in our whole army to carry those heights if they are well defended.

Col. Rush C. Hawkins, Union brigade commander

The Almighty will get tired of helping [Stonewall] Jackson after a while, and then he'll get the d—ndest thrashing—and the shoe pinches, for I shall get my share and probably all the blame, for the people will never blame Stonewall for any disaster.

Confederate Maj. Gen. A. P. Hill, corps commander

[**I**t was] the most impressive exhibition of military force, by all odds, which I ever witnessed. The whole Federal army had broken up their camps. . . . Over 100,000 infantry were visible, standing apparently in great solid squares upon the hilltops, for a space of three miles.

Confederate Lt. Col. Edward Porter Alexander, artillery commander, 1st Corps

The bombardment [of Fredericksburg] was kept up for over an hour, and no tongue or pen can describe the dreadful scene. . . . [N]othing in war can exceed the horror of that hour.

Pvt. James M. Dinkins, 18th Mississippi Infantry

Where men fell and left a vacant place other men stepped into their places and although death stared us in the face there was not a man who faltered.

Pvt. Josiah F. Murphey, 20th Massachusetts Infantry

How beautifully they came on! Their bright bayonets glistening in the sunlight made the line look like a huge serpent of blue and steel. . . . We could see out shells bursting in their ranks, making great gaps; but on they came, as though they would go straight through and over us.

Confederate Lt. William M. Owen, Washington Artillery

On the hill and slope behind and among us the sight is horrible and heartrending; hundreds of the bleeding and mangled are dragging themselves from the dead and dying, are trampled upon by the thousands, many of whom in the excitement hardly knew whither they were going save to certain slaughter.

Pvt. William Kepler, 4th Ohio Infantry

Men who had never seen a battle before, had never seen Confederate troops in action, raised that Confederate yell that seemed to be a part of the nature of the Confederate troops.

Lt. Col. Hamilton C. Jones, 57th North Carolina Infantry

Cheer up, my hearties! Cheer up! This is something we must all get used to. Remember, this brigade has never been whipped, and don't let it be whipped to-day.

Brig. Gen. Nathan Kimball, Union brigade commander

General, if you put every man now on the other side of the Potomac on that field to approach me over the same line and give me plenty of ammunition, I will kill them all before they reach my line. Look to your right. You are in some danger there, but not on my line.

Lt. Gen. James Longstreet, December 13, 1862,
replying to a warning from Robert E. Lee that the
Federal army at Fredericksburg was massing against
Longstreet's corps

A chicken could not live in that field when we open on it.

Confederate Lt. Col. Edward Porter Alexander,
artillery commander, First Corps

I have been in many engagements before but I never saw in my life such a slaughter.

Confederate Sgt. William R. Montgomery,
Cobb's Brigade

As I witnessed one line swept away by one fearful blast from Kershaw's men behind the stone wall, I forgot they were enemies and only remembered that they were men, and it is hard to see in cold blood brave men die.

Pvt. Alexander Hunter, 17th Virginia Infantry

We will whip them but gain no fruits of victory.

Confederate Gen. Thomas J. "Stonewall" Jackson,
Fredericksburg, 1862

It is well that war is so terrible—we should grow too fond of it.

Robert E. Lee, Fredericksburg, December 13, 1862

The Marye house marked the center of the Confederate line on the heights overlooking Fredericksburg. A sunken road was just below the house and provided 2,000 Southerners with a natural rifle pit in front of the Union line. Lee suffered 1,200 casualties; Burnside lost 7,000 men.

A series of braver, more desperate charges than those hurled against the troops in the sunken road was never known, and the piles and cross-piles of dead marked a field such as I never saw before or since.

Lt. Gen. James Longstreet

I not only wish them all dead but I wish them all in Hell.

Confederate Gen. Jubal Anderson Early, referring to the Federal army, December 15, 1862

Dear Mother, the fearful battle of Fredericksburg is over. The slaughter is terrible. The result is disastrous. Until we have good generals, it is useless to fight battles. Our real loss is far greater than reported in the newspapers.

Henry Hastings Curran, 146th New York Infantry

If there is a worse place than Hell, I am in it.

Abraham Lincoln, upon hearing of the Union disaster at Fredericksburg, December 1862

The Rebel position was unassailable. It was a perfect slaughter path and column after column was broken against it. It was not a battle. It was a wholesale slaughter of human beings sacrificed to the blind ambition and incapacities of some parties.

Union Capt. D. P. Conyngham

It can hardly be in human nature for men to show more valor, or generals to manifest less judgment.

Anonymous Northern reporter at Fredericksburg

The destruction of life has been fearful, and nothing gained.

Capt. William J. Nagle, 88th New York Infantry

We are now on the brink of destruction. It appears to me that the Almighty is against us.

Abraham Lincoln, December 1862

I hold that rebellion is treason, and that treason, persisted in, is death.

Union Gen. Benjamin F. Butler, December 24, 1862

Once let the black man get upon his person the brass letters, U.S.; let him get an eagle on his button, and a musket on his shoulder and bullets in his pocket, and there is no power on earth which can deny that he has earned the right to citizenship.

Frederick Douglass

To separate & destroy families & friends & mar the purest joys & happiness God has granted us in this world. To fill our hearts with hatred instead of love for our neighbours & to devastate the fair face of this beautiful world . . . what a cruel thing war is.

Robert E. Lee, December 25, 1862

So great is my confidence in General Lee that I am willing to follow him blindfolded.

Confederate Gen. Thomas J. "Stonewall" Jackson

Brave men die in battle.

Union Gen. William Starke Rosecrans, December 31, 1862, after the battle of Stones River, Tennessee

4

God Bless the Cause

Emancipation to Vicksburg

At a crossroads in Virginia known as Chancellorsville during the first days of May 1863, "Fighting Joe" Hooker's army outnumbered his Confederate adversaries by nearly two to one. Holding one-third of his army in reserve, the Union general led a third of his men up the Rappahannock River and across the Rapidan to strike at the left flank of Robert E. Lee's army. The remaining third was to provide a diversionary attack on Fredericksburg to keep the Confederates in their works.

Despite the disparity in numbers, Lee attacked Hooker, sending Stonewall Jackson's corps on a flanking march that surprised the right side of the Union line. Hooker himself was stunned during the fighting, and his men fell back to the Rapidan River. The Federal assault on Fredericksburg, however, broke through the Rebel line, but Lee left a portion of his army at Chancellorsville and attacked the advancing Yankees at Salem Church. Two days later the Union army pulled back, leaving Lee with his greatest victory and leaving Hooker as yet another castoff in a succession of frustrated Federal commanders.

Although the Yankees were driven back across the Rappahannock, the victorious Confederates suffered an irreplaceable loss when Jackson, Lee's chief lieutenant, was struck down by a volley from his own troops. He died one week later, not from his wound, but from pneumonia. He was replaced in the field by J. E. B. "Jeb" Stuart, whose success in the battle has often been overlooked.

The loss of Jackson would be sorely felt that summer when the Army of Northern Virginia again invaded Northern soil, this time penetrating into Pennsylvania. Its progress was also hampered by the absence of Stuart's cavalry, which was assigned to screen the movement of the army from Yankee cavalry and gather supplies, but whose absence also deprived Lee of reliable information regarding the location and strength of Union forces relative to the Southern advance.

Alerted to the Confederate incursion, Hooker maneuvered his army between Lee and the Federal capital and then resigned over a tiff with Maj. Gen. Henry Halleck, the general in chief. Maj. Gen. George Gordon Meade reluctantly accepted command of the Army of the Potomac just days before leading it into the greatest battle ever fought in the Western Hemisphere—Gettysburg.

Federal sacrifices during the first day of the fighting succeeded in securing a defensible position and allowed the Union army sufficient time to deploy in the area. For the next two days the Confederates attacked the right, left, and center of the Union line but failed to break through. Col. Joshua Lawrence Chamberlain's courageous defense of Little Round Top on July 2, 1863, proved a signal moment for Northern fortunes as much as Gen. George Pickett's ill-fated charge the following day spelled doom for the South. The thwarted charge exhausted Lee's army, and the Confederates retreated back to Virginia. The victory at Gettysburg renewed Northern hopes in the waning effort to preserve the Union. It proved to be the point after which the Confederate "high tide" slowly ebbed away.

Contemporaneous with the earthshaking events in Pennsylvania, the situation in the West also reached a climax when, after a siege of thirty-seven days, the key river town of Vicksburg, Mississippi, capitulated to U. S. Grant's army on July 4, 1864. The fall of Vicksburg effectively divided the Confederacy in two, isolating the Trans-Mississippi Department—Arkansas, Texas, and Louisiana—from the East and ensuring the eventual ruin of the secessionists' cause.

A most remarkable structure that human eyes ever rested upon. That man Haupt has built a bridge across Potomac Creek, . . . over which loaded trains are running every hour, and, upon my word, gentlemen, . . . [t]here is nothing in it but beanpoles and cornstalks.

Abraham Lincoln

Both sides quickly learned the value of railroads in transporting men and supplies to the front. Likewise, both learned to tear up track, burn bridges, and destroy equipment as ways of hobbling the other's line of supply. On the Union side, Herman Haupt (left) was appointed chief of construction and transportation for the U.S. Military Railroad. One of his first challenges was to restore the Pohick Creek bridge (right) whose span was 400 feet over the Potomac River. Lincoln visited the site and pondered how beanpoles and cornstalks could support a locomotive. Haupt's men would rebuild the bridge three times before the war's end.

It cannot be ignored. . . . The construction of railroads has introduced a new and very important element in war . . . for concentrating at particular positions, large masses of troops from remote sections . . . creating new strategic points and lines of operation.

Gen. George B. McClellan

If this war has developed some of the most brutal, bestial and devilish qualities lurking in the human race, it has also shown how much of the angel there is in the best men and women.

Mary Livermore, 1863

You have not conquered the South. You never will. War for the Union was abandoned; war for the Negro openly begun and with stronger battalions than before. With what success? Let the dead at Fredericksburg . . . answer.

Union Ohio Congressman Clement Vallandigham

My plans are perfect. May God have mercy on General Lee for I will have none.

Union Maj. Gen. Joseph E. Hooker, April 1862

And upon this act, sincerely believed to be an act of justice, warranted by the Constitution, upon military necessity, I invoke the considerable judgment of mankind, and the gracious favor of Almighty God.

Abraham Lincoln, Emancipation Proclamation, January 1, 1863

General: I have placed you at the head of the Army of the Potomac. . . . I have heard, in such a way as to believe it, of your recently saying that both the Army and the Government needed a Dictator. Of course it was not *for* this, but in spite of it, that I have given you the command. Only those generals who gain successes can set up dictators. What I now ask of you is military successes, and I will risk the dictatorship.

> *Abraham Lincoln, to Union Maj. Gen. Joseph E. Hooker, April 1862*

The Institute will be heard from today.

> *Confederate Gen. Thomas J. "Stonewall" Jackson, referring to the number of Virginia Military Institute graduates on his staff and within the ranks of his brigade*

All that May morning was marked by a strange quiet which settled down upon the corps as the soldiers rested in the line.

> *Lt. Hartwell Osborn, 35th Ohio Infantry*

For months following the battle of Fredericksburg, the two sides stared at each other over the remnants of the bridges that had spanned the Rappahannock. Photographer A. J. Russell captured this image (facing page) before the fighting resumed at Fredericksburg in May 1863.

As the men had been informed that Lee was running away, they had taken things easy, were lying about in groups and smoking pipes, or were looking for the best places to sleep in peace and comfort that night.

Lt. Frederick Otto von Fritsch, staff officer,
Schimmelfennig's Brigade, Union 11th Corps

God will not take him from us now that we need him so much.

Confederate Gen. Robert E. Lee, on the wounding of
Stonewall Jackson at Chancellorsville, May 3, 1863

A perfect sea of fire was in our faces from the many cannon parked around the Chancellor House and graping in all directions but the rear. Lee on the one side and Stuart on the other had closed upon the enemy, their wings joining just in front of the house.

Lt. D. Augustus Dickert, 3d South Carolina Infantry

Hooker's plan was to attack Lee on both flanks simultaneously from Chancellorsville
and Fredericksburg. The Confederate commander, however, split his army into three
parts to defend Fredericksburg and attack Hooker's flanks at Chancellorsville. The
audacity of Lee crippled Hooker's army and sent it reeling back in defeat, but the
price of victory cost Lee his greatest commander. Stonewall Jackson was mortally
wounded by his own men during the fighting. The battery pictured above was
deployed at Fredericksburg. The two images on the following pages depict the usual
aftermath of battle, burial of the dead and treating the wounded. In the second
image, the Marye house was used as a hospital for Union casualties.

123

The Chancellorsville campaign was over, and a tired, disappointed, disgusted army had nothing for the present to do but to wend its way back to its old camping grounds.

Lt. Porter Farley, 140th New York Infantry

To tell the truth, I just lost confidence in Joe Hooker.
Union Maj. Gen. Joseph E. Hooker

Numbers have now no terror for the Southern people. They are willing to wage war against quadruple their number.

John Jones, clerk, Confederate War Department, May 9, 1863

No description of what we have endured or what we have seen could give the slightest idea of the horrible truth.

Lt. Col. David R. E. Winn, 4th Georgia Infantry

Jackson died but his memory lived in the hearts of the soldiers, and on many a subsequent hard-fought field, I heard them exclaim, "Oh, for another Jackson!"

Confederate Gen. James H. Lane

In the midst of this awful scene, General Lee . . . rode to the front of his advancing battalions. His presence was the signal for one of those outbursts of enthusiasm which none can appreciate who have not witnessed them. . . . I thought that it must have been from such a scene that men in ancient days rose to the dignity of gods.

Maj. Charles Marshall, aide on Lee's staff

Hooker's career is exemplified by that of a rocket, he went up like one and came down like a stick.

Capt. George Armstrong Custer, Union 1st Cavalry

My God! My God! What will the country say?

Abraham Lincoln, responding to the news of the Union defeat at Chancellorsville, May 6, 1863

My men had no camps. . . . They would scatter for safety and gather at my call like Children of the Mist.

Confederate Maj. John S. Mosby

We cannot help beating them if we have the man. How much depends in military matters on one master mind!

Abraham Lincoln, June 1863

[The problem] resolved itself into a choice of one of two things: either to retire to Richmond and stand a siege, which must ultimately have ended in surrender, or to invade Pennsylvania.

Confederate Gen. Robert E. Lee, June 1863

I don't know whether I'm standing on my head or feet.

Union Gen. Joseph E. Hooker, June 1863

I am moving at once against Lee. A battle will decide the fate of our country and our cause. Pray earnestly, pray for the success of my country.

> *Maj. Gen. George Gordon Meade, commander,*
> *Army of the Potomac*

They will attack you in the morning and they will come booming—skirmishers three deep. You will have to fight like the devil until supports arrive.

> *Union Gen. John Buford, Gettysburg, July 1, 1863*

The enemy is advancing in strong force. I will fight him inch by inch, and if driven into the town I will barricade the streets and hold him back as long as possible.

> *Union Gen. John Reynolds, Gettysburg, July 1, 1863*

The enemy is here, and if we do not whip him, he will whip us.

> *Confederate Gen. Robert E. Lee, announcing his plans*
> *to attack the Federal army at Gettysburg, July 1, 1863*

Gettysburg, Pennsylvania, was a simple farming community that had grown up around the intersection of nine roads, five of which were major thoroughfares, making it a strategic commercial hub. Prior to the battle, the town was known primarily as the home of Pennsylvania College and the Lutheran Theological Seminary (pictured above). Classes were in session when the fighting began, but the students were dismissed quickly as the sounds of battle advanced toward the town. Both facilities were used by Confederates and Federals as observation posts and hospitals.

F orward! For God's sake, forward!

> *Gen. John Reynolds, before being mortally wounded,*
> *Gettysburg, July 1, 1863*

T ell [Maj. Gen. Abner] Doubleday to fight on the left, and I will fight on the right.

> *Maj. Gen. Oliver O. Howard,*
> *Union 11th Corps commander*

I think they fight harder in their own Country than they do in Virginia. I had rather fight them in Virginia then here, for we had to leave a great many of our wounded in the hands of the yankees.

> *Cpl. Sidney J. Richardson, 21st Georgia Infantry*

I 'm as dead a man as Julius Caesar.

> *Brig. Gen. Stephen H. Weed, Union brigade*
> *commander, mortally wounded at Little Round Top*

White-winged peace didn't roost at Little Round Top that night! There was not a man there that cared a snap for the golden rule, or that could have remembered one line of the Lord's Prayer. Both sides were whipped, and all were furious about it.

Sgt. Valerius C. Giles, 4th Texas Infantry

Hold that ground [Little Round Top] at all hazards.

Union Col. Strong Vincent to Union Col. Joshua Lawrence Chamberlain

The heroic energy of my officers could avail us no more. Our gallant line writhed & shrunk before the fire it could not repel. It was too evident that we could maintain the defensive no longer. As a last desperate resort, I ordered a charge.

Union Col. Joshua Lawrence Chamberlain, Twentieth Maine, Little Round Top, Gettysburg, July 2, 1863

At times I saw around me more of the enemy than my own men. Gaps, openings, swelling, closing again with convulsive energy. In the midst of this struggle our ammunition utterly failed. Half my left wing already lay on the field. . . . The words "Fix bayonets!" flew from man to man. The click of the steel seemed to give new zeal to all. The men dashed forward with a shout. . . . Our loss is terrible, but we are beating the Rebels as they were never beaten before.

> *Union Col. Joshua Lawrence Chamberlain, Little Round Top, Gettysburg, July 2, 1863*

We ran like a herd of wild cattle.

> *Confederate Col. William C. Oates, Little Round Top, Gettysburg, July 2, 1863*

An officer fired his pistol at my head with one hand while he handed me his sword with the other.

> *Union Col. Joshua Lawrence Chamberlain, Little Round Top, Gettysburg, July 2, 1863*

Tell my wife I am shot, but we fought like hell.

Confederate Gen. William Barksdale, Gettysburg, July 2, 1863

We were in this wheat field and the grain stood almost breast high. The Rebs had their slight protection, but we were in the open, without a thing better than a wheat straw to catch a Minnie bullet.

Lt. Charles A. Fuller, 61st New York Infantry

I have been a soldier all my life. I have commanded companies. I have commanded regiments. I have commanded divisions. And I have commanded even more. But there are no fifteen thousand men in the world that can go across that ground.

Confederate Gen. James Longstreet, July 3, 1863, arguing with Lee against what became known as Pickett's Charge

There is the enemy, and there I mean to attack him.

Confederate Gen. Robert E. Lee, July 3, 1863

I don't want to make this attack. I believe it will fail. I do not see how it can succeed. I would not make it now but that General Lee has ordered it and expects it.

> *Confederate Gen. James Longstreet, referring to Pickett's Charge*

Never will I forget those scenes and sounds. The earth seems unsteady beneath this furious cannonading, and the air might be said to be agitated by the wings of death.

> *Capt. John E. Dooley, 1st Virginia Infantry*

Come on boys! Give them the cold steel! Who will follow me?

> *Gen. Lewis A. Armistead, Confederate brigade commander, during Pickett's Charge*

There are times when a corps commander's life does not count.

> *Union Gen. Winfield Scott Hancock, Gettysburg, July 3, 1863*

P. F. Rothermel was commissioned by the state of Pennsylvania to portray Pickett's Charge (above). The artist placed Gen. George G. Meade, the Union commander and a Pennsylvanian, on the extreme left of the canvas, despite the fact that Meade was not at the scene of the charge. The focus of the painting, however, is on the average soldier, who has been highlighted in the middle of the canvas by his bright undershirt. Interestingly, all the soldiers seem to favor one another.

Thure de Thulstrup's depiction of the charge focused on the back of the Union line (facing page), and the artist positioned Union Gen. Winfield Scott Hancock in the foreground, directing the placement of an artillery limber toward the small stone wall sheltering the front line of his troops. Hancock was wounded during the fighting but refused to leave the field until the charge had been repelled.

136

I could see long streaks of light through the rebel columns, but they went forward. I was afraid they would capture our guns, but all of a sudden they seemed to melt away as our infantry opened on them, and then we could hear the Northern cheer.

Sgt. James P. Sullivan, 6th Wisconsin Infantry

My grand old division, which was so full of faith and courage then, is now almost extinguished. But one field-officer in the whole command escaped in that terible third of July slaughter, and alas! alas! for the men who fearlessly followed their lead on to certain death.

Maj. Gen. George E. Pickett, Confederate division commander

When news of the battle at Gettysburg reached Washington, the town's two foremost photographers personally led teams to the site. The first to arrive, Alexander Gardner, departed for the battlefield on July 3 and was temporarily detained by retreating Confederates on July 4. His team arrived in Gettysburg on July 5, the first photographers on the scene, but there was no one to guide them around the field, to reconstruct what had happened. He focused on the unburied dead, scenes of the battlefield, the town, and the cemetery. Two samples of these appear on the facing and following pages.

Mathew Brady, however, did not travel to Gettysburg until more than a week after Gardner had returned. By then he found several guides available, and his photographers concentrated on specific sites that had become well known to the public over the weeks since the conclusion of the battle. Brady included himself in most of these photographs, such as the image of the cemetery gate below, as a representative of the general public.

It's all my fault. It is I who have lost this fight, and you must help me out of it the best way you can. All good men must rally. . . . Never let them see you run.

> *Confederate Gen. Robert E. Lee, after the repulse of Pickett's Charge*

It is all over now. Many of us are prisoners, many are dead, many wounded, bleeding and dying. Your soldier lives and mourns and but for you, my darling, he would rather be back there with his dead, to sleep for all time in an unknown grave.

> *Maj. Gen. George E. Pickett, Confederate division commander*

Victory! Waterloo Eclipsed!

> Philadelphia Inquirer *announcing the Union victory at Gettysburg*

This is the darkest day of the war.

> *John Jones, clerk, Confederate War Department, July 8, 1863*

My pen is heavy, O, you dead, who at Gettysburg have baptized with your blood the second birth of Freedom in America, how you are to be envied! I rise from a grave whose wet clay I have passionately kissed, and I look up and see Christ spanning the battle-field with his feet, and reaching fraternal and loving up to Heaven. His right hand opens the gates of Paradise,—with his left he sweetly beckons to these mutilated, bloody, swollen forms to ascend.

New York Times *correspondent Samuel Wilkeson, whose son Bayard was killed on July 2, 1863*

The charm of Robert Lee's invincibility is broken. The Army of the Potomac . . . has stood nobly up to its terrible work in spite of its long disheartening list of hard-fought failures.

George Templeton Strong

The army has laboured hard, endured much & behaved nobly. . . . I fear I required of it impossibilities. But it responded to the call nobly and cheerfully, and though it did not win a victory it conquered a success. We must now prepare for harder blows and harder work.

> *Confederate Gen. Robert E. Lee, in a letter to his wife, Mary, after the battle of Gettysburg*

Our Army held the war in the hollow of their hand and they would not close it.

> *Abraham Lincoln, speaking of Meade's failure to follow up the victory at Gettysburg*

See what a lot of land these fellows hold, of which Vicksburg is the key. . . . Let us get Vicksburg and all that country is ours. The war can never be brought to a close until that key is in our pocket.

Abraham Lincoln

This is a death struggle and will be terrible.

Maj. Gen. William Tecumseh Sherman, Union corps commander

Now commenced a strange spectacle in this thrilling drama of war. Flags [of truce] were displayed along both lines, and the troops thronged the breastworks, gaily chatting with each other; discussing the issues of war; disputing over differences of opinion, losses in fights, etc. Numbers of the Confederates accepted invitations to visit the enemy's lines, where they were hospitably entertained and warmly welcomed. They were abundantly supplied with provisions and supplies of various kinds.

Pvt. William H. Tunnard, 3d Louisiana Infantry

There were many assaults against the Confederate line at Vicksburg during the forty-seven-day siege, but the costliest occurred on May 22, 1863. The attack was prefaced by a four-hour barrage from every Federal battery and gunboat. Seemingly countless columns of Yankee soldiers rushed forward at 10 A.M., but Confederate fire shredded them. Several flags were planted on the parapets, but the success was short-lived. Southern canister and musketfire kept the Northerners pinned down throughout the afternoon. There was no breakthrough. Instead, it was the bloodiest day of the Vicksburg campaign with almost 3,200 Union casualties; Rebel losses were less than 500. The Thulstrup painting above depicts the assault on Fort Beauregard, one of the places in the Confederate line where the color-bearer placed his banner atop the earthworks.

I know my people [Northerners]. I know their peculiar weaknesses and their national vanity; I know we can get better terms from them on the Fourth of July than on any other day of the year.

> *Confederate Gen. John Pemberton, a native of*
> *Pennsylvania and commanding general at Vicksburg,*
> *July 3, 1863*

The fate of the Confederacy was sealed when Vicksburg fell. Much hard fighting was to be done afterwards and many precious lives were to be sacrificed; but the morale was with the supporters of the Union ever after.

> *Union Gen. Ulysses S. Grant*

The Father of Waters again goes unvexed to the sea. . . . Peace does not appear so distant as it did. I hope it will come soon, and come to stay; and so come as to be worth the keeping in all future time.

> *Abraham Lincoln, on the fall of Vicksburg,*
> *August 26, 1863*

We recognized an honorable foe. . . . Many a ration was divided, many a canteen filled, and many were the mutual, sympathizing wishes that the cruel war might soon be over.

Lt. Samuel H. M. Byers, 5th Iowa Infantry

Yesterday we rode on the pinnacle of success—today, absolute ruin seems to be our portion. The Confederacy totters to its destruction.

Josiah Gorgas, Confederate chief of ordnance, July 1863

There will be some black men who can remember that, with silent tongue, and clenched teeth, and a steady eye, and well-poised bayonet, they have helped mankind on to this great consummation; while, I fear, there will be some white ones, unable to forget that, with malignant heart, and deceitful speech, they have strove to hinder it.

Abraham Lincoln, August 26, 1863

They tell me some of you will take back the Proclamation; don't do it. When you are dead and in Heaven, in a thousand years that action of yours will make the Angels sing your praises, I know it.

> *Hannah Johnson, mother of a soldier in the 54th*
> *Massachusetts, in a letter to Lincoln, July 31, 1863*

War ennobles the age. We do not often have a moment of grandeur in these hurried, slipshod lives, but the behavior of the young men has taught us much. We will not again disparage America, now that we have seen what men it will bear.

> *Ralph Waldo Emerson, 1863*

This year has brought about many changes that at the beginning were or would have been thought impossible. The close of the year finds me a soldier for the cause of my race. May God bless the cause, and enable me in the coming year to forward it on.

> *Christopher Fleetwood, free black from Baltimore, 1863*

5

We Are Going to Be Wiped Off the Earth

Chickamauga to Lincoln's Second Inauguration

Dᴇꜱᴘɪᴛᴇ ᴅᴇꜰᴇᴀᴛꜱ at Gettysburg and Vicksburg, Southern will and determination guaranteed that hostilities would continue for almost two more years, but the South's prosecution of the war shifted strategy. With the ranks of the army greatly diminished by two years of fighting, the situation in the field demanded a defensive posture. Many believed that a stout resistance would drain the Union's resolve to carry on the war and lead to the peaceful separation they desired. Losing men and materiél they could ill-afford to replace, Southerners prayed that Lincoln would be defeated in the 1864 election by former Gen. George B. McClellan, a "Peace Democrat" who would almost certainly end the war diplomatically.

When a Union army under William S. Rosecrans attacked the Confederate Army of Tennessee's last formidable line of defense in the West, concentrated around Chattanooga, the Rebels fell back into northern Georgia. There the Southern army received reinforcements and broke the Union line in one of the few battles of the war in which Rebel forces held numerical superiority. The battle of Chickamauga (September 19–20, 1863) was a Confederate victory, but the Southern commander, Braxton Bragg, failed to exploit his advantage and allowed Rosecrans to regroup and retrench in Chatanooga. At this critical time, Lincoln chose to replace Rosecrans with U. S. Grant, who he knew would accept nothing less than success. Under Grant's direction, the Federals broke out from Chattanooga and drove the Rebels from the area on November 23–25.

In March 1864 Grant was promoted to lieutenant general and given command of all Union armies. Under his guidance a plan for a coordinated Federal offensive was implemented. In the East, he would attack

Robert E. Lee and the Army of Northern Virginia, and in the West, William Tecumseh Sherman would target the Army of Tennessee. Later Grant authorized Phil Sheridan to initiate a campaign in the Shenandoah Valley, and Benjamin Butler coordinated Union troops on the Virginia Peninsula prior to the siege of Petersburg.

In the East, before Grant was ready to attack, Lee attacked at the Wilderness, momentarily thwarting the Union offensive. Rather than fall back like so many other Federal armies had done earlier, Grant's army harassed the Southerners across the Virginia countryside in a gritty war of attrition. Tens of thousands died at Spotsylvania Court House, Yellow Tavern, Cold Harbor, and Trevilian Station before Grant maneuvered his army toward the James River and Petersburg and a siege that would doom Lee's Confederates.

In the West, Sherman's steady advance into Georgia eventually targeted Atlanta and besieged the city. When the Army of Tennessee abandoned the vital transportation center, Northern troops moved in and occupied the city. Realizing that he had an opportunity to strike fear throughout the South, Sherman devised a plan to March to the Sea from Atlanta to Savannah and then march through the Carolinas in a campaign of total war that foraged liberally off the land, damaging or destroying homes and farms and confiscating livestock and anything else that might contribute to the Confederate war effort.

Politically, Lincoln's chances for reelection rose and fell with the war news. Grant's losses were staggering, and Sherman's army was slugging its way into the Deep South. Nevertheless, Lincoln carried the November election, aided by the support of "War Democrats," the ballots of Union soldiers, and the timely news of the fall of Atlanta.

I would make this war as severe as possible, and show no symptoms of tiring till the South begs for mercy.

Maj. Gen. William Tecumseh Sherman,
September 17, 1863

There are thousands of men in the prime of life who this morning thought they were destined to live to a ripe old age who tonight are lying on the battlefield stark and stiff and who will be covered where they fell with a few shovels full of dirt and left to rot with nothing to mark the place where a hero perished for his country and that the government might live.

Cpl. William B. Miller, 75th Indiana Infantry,
Chickamauga

We rose up as one man and poured into them such a volley from our faithful Enfields as to make many of them bite the dust for the last time.

Pvt. John T. Coxe, 2d South Carolina Infantry,
Chickamauga

Never in any battle I had witnessed was there such a discharge of cannon and musketry. . . . [T]he first thing I saw was General Rosecrans crossing himself—he was a very devout Catholic. "Hello!" I said to myself, "if the general is crossing himself, we are in a desperate situation."

> *Charles H. Dana, assistant U.S. secretary of war,*
> *Chickamauga*

With a wild yell the Confederates swept on far to their left. They seemed everywhere victorious. Rosecrans was borne back in the retreat. . . . He concluded that . . . the next stand must be made at Chattanooga.

> *Lt. Col. Gates P. Thruston, staff officer, Union 20th*
> *Corps commanded by Maj. Gen. Alexander McCook*

The Major gave orders to fix bayonets, which was promptly obeyed, but when the order was given to "forward march," not a man moved.

> *Capt. Isaac Cusac, 21st Ohio Infantry, Chickamauga*

Our opponents finally began lowering their guns, which we took and threw behind us. Then at once we became friends and began a frenzied trading of tobacco for coffee.

Pvt. James M. Weiser, 54th Virginia Infantry, Chickamauga

It seems to me that the *élan* of the Southern soldier was never seen after Chickamauga—that brillant dash which had distinguished him was gone forever.

Lt. Gen. Daniel H. Hill, Confederate corps commander, Chickamauga

We was in a fight last saterday and last sunday. our redgement was badley cut up. . . . we have now fell back on Chattanuga and are bisy fortifing. . . . thay have a larger force than we have but we will Whip them or die atriing.

Pvt. Benjamin Mabrey, 82d Indiana Infantry, Chickamauga

Bragg is not the genral that Lee is and the western army cant fight like the virginia army. if genral Lee was hear he would have had the yankees drove out of Tennesee.

> *Cpl. Milton Barrett, 3d Battalion Georgia*
> *Sharpshooters, Chickamauga*

You have played the part of a damn scoundrel, and are a coward, and if you were any part of a man I would slap your jaws and force you to resent it. . . . I say to you that if you ever again try to interfere with me or cross my path it will be at the peril of your life.

> *Gen. Nathan Bedford Forrest, September 1863, to Gen.*
> *Braxton Bragg for failing to follow up the victory at*
> *Chickamauga and for restructuring elements of*
> *Forrest's command*

[They] must now see the impossibility of subjugating the Southern people.

> *John Jones, clerk, Confederate War Department,*
> *speaking on the Confederate victory at Chickamauga,*
> *September 1863*

[The enemy] did not fire on us nor seem to be disturbed by our presence. . . . But, I suppose, they looked upon the garrison of Chattanooga as prisoners of war, feeding or starving themselves, and thought it would be inhuman to kill any of them except in self-defense.

Gen. Ulysses S. Grant, Chattanooga

Weuns thought youns was coming out for a review, we didn't think youns was coming out to fight weuns.

Confederate prisoner after the fighting at Orchard Knob

Now, boys, lie low, you know, and let 'em come up close, you know, and then rise up and give 'em hell, you know.

Maj. Gen. Philip H. Sheridan, Union division commander, during the fighting at Lookout Mountain

This was one of the few times in battle that it took a braver man to run than it did to stand; because those who remained behind the rocks could surrender in safety, and those who ran would draw the fire of the heavy Yankee line.

Pvt. John W. Simmons, 27th Mississippi Infantry, Lookout Mountain

The taking of Missionary Ridge, therefore, was inaugurated not so much by the genius of commanders, or the bravery of soldiers, as by a mistake.

Union chaplain John J. Hight, Missionary Ridge

We are now in the darkest hour of our political existence.

Jefferson Davis, after the fall of Chattanooga, November 1863

I felt sorry for General Bragg. . . . [T]he soldiers would raise the yell, . . . "Bully for Bragg, he's h—l on retreat."

> *Pvt. Sam Watkins, 1st Tennessee Infantry, recalling the retreat from Chattanooga*

War is simply power restrained by the constitution or compact.

> *Maj. Gen. William Tecumseh Sherman, January 31, 1864*

Liberty once lost will never be recovered without blood.

> *Confederate Vice President Alexander H. Stephens, March 12, 1864*

In peace there is a beautiful harmony in all the departments of life—they all fit together like a Chinese puzzle, but in war all is ajar. Nothing fits, and it is the struggle between the stronger and weaker, and the latter, however much it may appeal to the better feelings of our nature, must kick the beam. To make war we must and will harden our hearts.

> *Union Gen. William Tecumseh Sherman, April 21, 1864*

U pon the progress of our arms all else chiefly depends.

Abraham Lincoln, 1864

I had quite a talk with [Gen. George Gordon] Meade, who said among other things that Uncle Abe was very tender hearted about shooting a deserter, but that he was perfectly willling to sacrifice a thousand men in a useless fight.

Maj. Henry L. Abbott, 20th Massachusetts Infantry

L ee's army will be your objective point. Wherever Lee goes, there you will go also.

Gen. Ulysses S. Grant, March 1864

T he summer days are almost here when we shall be wearily plodding over the roads once more in search of *victory* or *death.* Many a poor fellow will find the latter. I dread the approaching campaign. I can see horrors insurmountable through the summer months.

Union Pvt. Robert G. Carter, April 26, 1964

If victorious, we have everything to live for.
If defeated, there will be nothing left to live for.

Confederate Gen. Robert E. Lee, May 4, 1864

The morning was still, scarce a sound was heard, as
the hours passed, that was not native to the woods.
. . . Indeed, in that Wilderness, in which a bird had
scarce heart to peep, there was, through all that
forenoon, something oppressive in the dim light and
the strange quiet.

Lt. Sartell Prentice, 12th U.S. Infantry

The instant the regiment showed itself and before it
was fairly out into the clearing a line of smoke puffed
from the edge of the woods opposite and a volley of
musketry sent its bullets into our ranks.

Capt. Porter Farley, 140th New York Infantry

Ulysses S. Grant was given command of all Union armies in 1864, and he initiated a
unified offensive in which William Tecumseh Sherman challenged the Army of Tennessee in the West while Grant and the Army of the Potomac engaged Lee and the
Army of Northern Virginia in the East. The image on the facing page is of a council of
war conducted at Massaponax, Virginia, during the Overland campaign. Grant is at the
extreme left, leaning over the pew and studying a map.

Face the fire and go in where it is hottest.

Confederate Gen. Ambrose Powell Hill, the Wilderness,
May 5, 1864

Scarce had we moved a step, when Gen. Lee, in
front of the whole command, raised himself in his
stirrups, uncovered his grey hairs, and with an
earnest, yet anxious voice, exclaimed above the din
and confusion of the hour, "*Texans always move
them.*" . . . Never before in my lifetime or since, did I
ever witness such a scene as was enacted when Lee
pronounced these words, with the appealing look he
gave. A yell rent the air that must have been heard
for miles around, and but few eyes in that old brigade
of veterans and heroes of many a bloody field was
undimmed by honest, heart-felt tears. [The man next
to me,] with tears coursing down his cheeks and yells
issuing from his throat exclaimed, "I would charge
hell itself for that old man."

Pvt. Robert Campbell, 5th Texas Infantry

I am heartily tired of hearing about what Lee is going to do. Some of you always seem to think he is suddenly going to turn a double somersault, and land in our rear and on both of our flanks at the same time. Go back to your command, and try to think what we are going to do ourselves, instead of what Lee is going to do.

> *Lt. Gen. Ulysses S. Grant, at the battle*
> *of the Wilderness, May 5, 1864*

In the darkness of the night, in the gloom of a tangled forest, and after men's nerves had been racked by the strain of a two days' desperate battle, the most immovable commander might have been shaken. But it was in just such emergencies that General Grant was always at his best.

> *Lt. Col. Horace Porter, aide on Grant's staff*

I saw two hundred wagons crowded with wounded men. The dark spot in the mud told all too plainly where some poor fellow's life had dripped out in those dreadful hours. While our soldiers fight, I can stand and feed and nurse them. My place is anywhere between the bullet and the battlefield.

> *Volunteer nurse Clara Barton,*
> *during the battle of the Wilderness*

Grant's military standing with the enlisted men this day hung on the direction we turned at the Chancellorsville House. If to the left, he was to be rated with Meade and Hooker and Burnside and Pope—the generals who preceded him. . . . [W]e turned to the right. Instantly all of us heard a sigh of relief. Our spirits rose. We marched freely. The men began to sing. The enlisted men understood the flanking movement. That night we were happy.

> *Pvt. Frank Wilkeson, New York Light Artillery*

Grant has gone to the Wilderness, crawled in, drawn up the ladder, and pulled in the hole after him, and I guess we'll have to wait till he comes out before we know just what he's up to.

> *Abraham Lincoln*

Lee is *not* retreating: he is a brave and skilful soldier and he will fight while he has a division or a day's ration left. These Rebels are not half-starved and ready to give up—a more sinewy, tawny, formidable-looking set of men could not be.

> *Lt. Col. Theodore Lyman, aide on Meade's staff*

I will not take my regiment in another such charge if Jesus Christ himself should order it!

> *Union Capt. Thomas E. Barker, at the Wilderness, June 2, 1864*

Go back! Go back! And do your duty, as I have done mine, and our country will be safe. Go back! Go back! I had rather die than be whipped.

> *Confederate Gen. J. E. B. "Jeb" Stuart, shouting encouragement to his troops after being mortally wounded at Yellow Tavern, May 11, 1864*

Follow Forrest to the death if it costs ten thousand lives and breaks the [Federal] treasury. There will be no peace in Tennessee till Forrest is dead.

> *Union Gen. William Tecumseh Sherman, June 1864*

We accepted this war for the worthy object . . . of restoring the national authority over the whole national domain . . . and the war will end when that object is attained. Under God, I hope it never will until that time.

Abraham Lincoln, June 16, 1864

We cannot change the hearts of those people of the South, but we can make war so terrible, make them so sick of war that generations would pass away before they would again appeal to it.

Union Gen. William Tecumseh Sherman, 1864

I see no bright spot anywhere. The blood and treasure spent on this summer's campaign have done little for the country.

George Templeton Strong, commenting on Grant's apparent lack of success, July 1864

I steadily believe that Grant is going to succeed, and that we shall have Richmond—but oh what a price to pay for it!

> *Walt Whitman, serving as a nurse in*
> *Washington, D.C., 1864*

I pledge you that my study is to accomplish peace and honor at as small a cost to life and property as possible . . . [and] that I will take infinitely more delight in curing the wounds made by war than by inflicting them.

> *Union Gen. William Tecumseh Sherman, 1864*

We are fighting for *independence,* and that, or extermination, we will have. . . . We will govern ourselves . . . if we have to see every Southern plantation sacked, and every Southern city in flames.

> *Jefferson Davis, July 17, 1864*

Grief and constant anxiety kill nearly as many women as men die on the battlefield.

Mary Boykin Chesnut

This war is eating my life out. I have a strong impression that I shall not live to see the end.

Abraham Lincoln, 1864

Damn the torpedoes! Full steam ahead!

Union Adm. David Farragut, Mobile Bay, Alabama, August 5, 1864

This morning, as for some time past, it seems exceedingly probable that this administration will not be re-elected. Then it will be my duty to so co-operate with the President elect, as to save the Union between the election and the inauguration; as he will have secured his election on such ground that he can not possibly save it afterwards.

Abraham Lincoln's "blind memorandum" to members of his cabinet, issued August 23, 1864

That every slave who escapes from the Rebel States is a loss to the Rebellion and a gain to the Loyal Cause I need not stop to argue . . . the proposition is self evident. The negro is the stomach of the rebellion.

Frederick Douglass to President Lincoln,
August 29, 1864

If slaves make good soldiers, our whole theory of slavery is wrong.

Confederate Gen. Howell Cobb, 1864

All that has gone before is mere skirmishing. The war now begins.

Gen. William Tecumseh Sherman, March 12, 1864

[Sherman] found us ready to receive his gay and awe-inspiring columns, who moved in perfect step, with banners flying and bands playing, as though he expected to charm us.

Lt. Lot D. Young, 4th Kentucky (C.S.) Infantry

As the soldiers caught the announcement that Atlanta was in sight, such a cheer went up as must have been heard even in the entrenchments of the doomed city itself.

Maj. James A. Connolly, 123d Illinois Infantry

Shot and shell rained in every direction. Great volumes of sulphurous smoke rolled over the town, trailing down to the ground, and through this stifling gloom the sun glared down like a red eye peering through a bronze colored cloud.

Wallace P. Reed of Atlanta, August 1864

I shall never forget the night we left Atlanta. The old rolling-mills were on fire, and four hundred bales of cotton belonging to old man Wells were burning. On going up a big hill below Atlanta the fire was blazing so brightly I could count the hairs in the horse's tail by its light.

Col. George W. Adair, on Hood's staff,
Army of Tennessee

When we passed through the enemy's works we saw how formidable they were. They had no less than three lines, two of them protected by the strongest kind of abatis. I do not think it would have been possible to have taken them by assault.

Sgt. Rice C. Bull, 123d New York Infantry

Glorious news this morning—Atlanta taken at last!!! . . . It is the greatest event of the war.

George Templeton Strong, September 3, 1864

They [Southerners] cannot be made to love us, but they may be made to fear us.

Gen. William Tecumseh Sherman, November 1864

We are going to be wiped off the earth.

Mary Boykin Chesnut, after the fall of Atlanta, 1864

175

If the North can march an army right through the South, it is proof positive that the North can prevail. . . . I will not attempt to send couriers back, but trust to the Richmond papers to keep you well advised. I can make this march and make Georgia howl!

Gen. William Tecumseh Sherman,
November 1864, to Grant

If you can whip Lee, and I can march to the Atlantic, I think Uncle Abe will give us twenty days' leave of absence to see the young folks.

Gen. William Tecumseh Sherman, November 1864,
communicating his plans to Grant prior to the
March to the Sea

Before abandoning Atlanta to begin the March to the Sea, Sherman's army was ordered to destroy everything of military value, including anything having to do with the railroads. In no time, his men became masters of destruction. In the photograph to the right, rails are placed over a bonfire, after which they will be bent around trees or telegraph poles. The results became known as "Sherman's bow-ties" and "Sherman's hairpins."

If this cause that's so near my heart is doomed to fail, I pray that heaven may let me fall with it, with my face toward the foe, and my arm battling for that which I know to be right.

Maj. Gen. Patrick R. Cleburne, Confederate division commander, October 4, 1864, six weeks before his death at the battle of Franklin, Tennessee

The truth is, the whole army is burning with an insatiable desire to wreak vengeance upon South Carolina. I almost tremble at her fate, but feel that she deserves all that seems to be in store for her.

Gen. William Tecumseh Sherman, 1864

I beg to present to you, as a Christmas gift, the city of Savannah.

Gen. William Tecumseh Sherman, in a telegram to Lincoln, December 1864

General Hood, if you were a whole man, I'd whip you within an inch of your life.

> *Gen. Nathan Bedford Forrest, November 30, 1864*

The [VMI] cadets, gallant little boys, were sent up to reënforce us, and no veterans ever behaved better than those brave little fellows (the flower of the South), and I remember how I thought it shameful to subject such youths to such a fire.

> *Sgt. Thomas H. Neilson, 62d Virginia Infantry,*
> *at New Market*

[Maj. Gen. Franz] Sigel seemed in a state of excitement and rode here and there with Stahel and Moor, all jabbering in German. In his excitement he seemed to forget his English entirely, and the purely American portion of his staff were totally useless to him.

> *Col. David H. Strother, staff officer to Sigel*

Our loss was terrible, while the Yankees lost but few. I only saw three dead Union soldiers and I did not see one that was wounded. . . . All that we could shoot at was the smoke from their guns, they were so well posted. It was called our victory, but it was a costly one.

Pvt. George W. Nichols, 61st Georgia Infantry,
at Monocacy, Maryland

We haven't taken Washington, but we've scared Abe Lincoln like hell!

Maj. Gen. Jubal Early, Confederate commander,
Army of the Valley, July 13, 1864

I want Sheridan put in command of all the troops in the field with instructions to put himself south of the enemy and follow him to the death.

Lt. Gen. Ulysses S. Grant following
Early's raids near Washington

Mosby has annoyed me considerably.

> *Gen. Philip H. Sheridan, Union commander,*
> *Army of the Shenandoah*

Hurrah for Mosby!

> *Gen. Robert E. Lee*

I never felt so bad in my life—I felt as though we were disgraced and had probably lost the day and cared little whether I was shot or not—only when I was going back I thought about being shot in the back and turned and walked backwards.

> *Lt. William H. Root, 75th New York Infantry,*
> *at Winchester*

All was as peaceful and quiet as though no sign of war would ever be seen in that peaceful valley again. Sheridan's army lay in quiet upon the beautiful fields, oblivious of the fact that a Rebel host in battle array was close upon it, and in an hour one of the most remarkable battles in the annals of war would be in progress.

Cpl. Clinton Beckwith, 121st New York Infantry,
at Cedar Creek

Such confusion, such panic, was never witnessed before by the troops. Our cannoneers got their guns in position, and enlivened the scene by throwing shell, grape, and cannister into the flying fugitives.

Capt. D. Augustus Dickert, 3d South Carolina Infantry

The rebel colors are in our rear and the brigade has given way on our right. Shall the "old Eighth" run? Yes, and at once, every man for himself and to his utmost, if he does not want to take his chances of testing the hospitality of some Southern prison.

Capt. Moses McFarland, 8th Vermont Infantry

As we debouched into the fields and passed around the wagons and through these groups [of retreating soldiers], the general would wave his hat to the men and point to the front, never lessening his speed as he pressed forward. It was enough; one glance at the eager face and familiar black horse and they knew him, and starting to their feet, they swung their caps around their heads and broke into cheers as [Sheridan] passed beyond them; and then, gathering up their belongings and shouldering their arms, they started after him for the front, shouting to the comrades further out in the fields, "Sheridan! Sheridan!" waving their hats, and pointing after him as he dashed onward; and they too comprehended instantly, for they took up the cheer and turned back for the battle-field.

Maj. George A. Forsyth, aide on Sheridan's staff

To one who had seen the rout and panic and loss of the morning, it seemed impossible that this was the same army. . . . As soon as the Confederate infantry was fully engaged with ours in the centre, the order was given for the cavalry divisions to charge both flanks of the enemy line. . . . The effect was magical. . . . [A]s the sun went down, the army which at daybreak had gained one of the most dramatic and overwhelming victories of the war was a frantic rabble, decimated in numbers, and flying before the same army it had twelve hours before so completely surprised and routed. . . . This ended the career of [Jubal] Early's army. As an army it never fought another battle,—its commander never again attempted to redeem the Shenandoah Valley, nor to invade the North.

Maj. A. Bayard Nettleton, 2d Ohio Calvary

This is the bulliest day since Christ was born.

Gen. George Armstrong Custer, Union 1st Cavalry, at Cedar Creek, Virginia, September 19, 1864

I found it impossible to rally the troops, they would not listen to entraties, threats, or appeals of any kind. A terror of the enemy's cavalry had seized them. The rout was as thorough and disgraceful as ever happened to our army.

> *Lt. Gen. Jubal A. Early,*
> *commander of the Army of the Valley*

Reduction to poverty brings prayers for peace more surely and more quickly than does the destruction of human life.

> *Gen. Philip Henry Sheridan*

I shall always respect War hereafter. The cost of life, the dreary havoc of comfort and time, are overpaid by the Vistas it opens of Eternal Life, Eternal Law, reconstructing and uplifting Society.

> *Ralph Waldo Emerson, September 26, 1864*

What will the aristocrats do, with a railsplitter for President, and a tailor for Vice President?

> *Vice President-Elect Andrew Johnson, November 1864*

Where Slavery is, there Liberty cannot be; and where Liberty is, there Slavery cannot be.

Sen. Charles Sumner, Massachusetts,
November 5, 1864

We are fighting for existence; and by fighting alone can independence be gained.

Jefferson Davis, 1864

The purpose of the people . . . to maintain the integrity of the Union, was never more firm, nor more nearly unanimous, than now. . . . We are gaining strength, and may, if need be, maintain the contest indefinitely.

Abraham Lincoln, December 6, 1864

If the Confederacy fails, there should be written on its tombstone, "Died of a theory."

Jefferson Davis, 1864

The darkest and most dismal day . . . a crisis such as not been experienced before.

> *John Jones, clerk, Confederate War Department, after the Southern defeat at Nashville, December 19, 1864*

The deep waters are closing over us.

> *Mary Boykin Chesnut, December 19, 1864*

Valor alone is relied upon now for our salvation. Every one thinks the Confederacy will at once gather up its military strength and strike such blows as will astonish the world.

> *John Jones, clerk, Confederate War Department, February 1865*

Shame—disgrace—misery. . . . The grand smash has come.

> *Mary Boykin Chesnut, February 25, 1865*

Both sides read the same Bible, and pray to the same God; and each invokes his aid against the other. It may seem strange that any men should dare to ask a just God's assistance in wringing their bread from the sweat of other men's faces; but let us judge not that we be not judged.

Abraham Lincoln, Second Inaugural Address, March 4, 1865

Fondly do we hope—fervently do we pray—that this mighty scourge of war may speedily pass away. Yet if God wills that it continue . . . so it must be said "the judgments of the Lord are true and righteous altogether."

Abraham Lincoln, Second Inaugural Address, March 4, 1865

With malice toward none; with charity for all; with firmness in the right, let us strive on to finish the work we are in; to bind up the nation's wounds . . . to do all which may achieve a just, and a lasting peace, among ourselves, and with all nations.

Abraham Lincoln, Second Inaugural Address, March 4, 1865

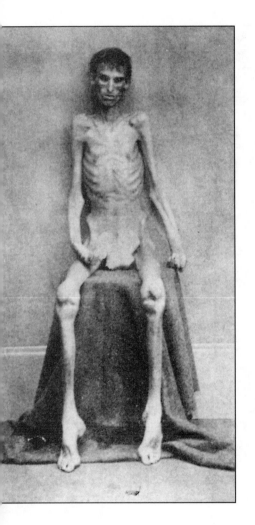

The released prisoners of war are now coming up from the Southern prisons. Can these be men? Were they really not mummied, dwindled corpses to endure the courses? They lay there with a horrible look in their eyes. Probably no more appalling sight was ever seen on this Earth.

Walt Whitman

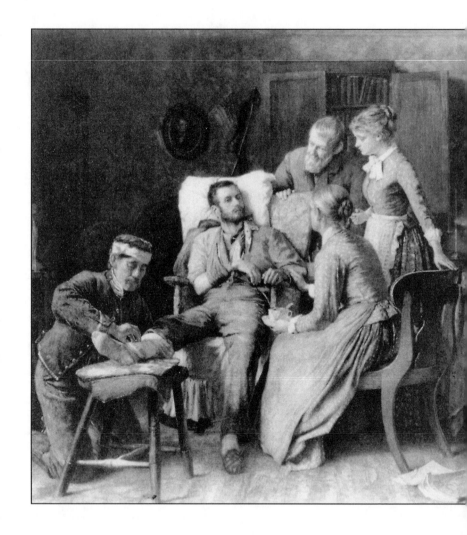

6

We Are All Americans

The Road to Appomattox

WHILE LINCOLN'S reelection dashed Confederate hopes of ending the war through political means, Southern leaders resolved to continue the fight, essentially postponing the inevitable. In June 1864 the Army of the Potomac began the longest sustained operation of the war, the ten-month siege of Petersburg.

The high casualties Grant had sustained at Cold Harbor earlier had convinced him to isolate Richmond by cutting the key railroad lines and roadways that supplied the city from Petersburg, a vital transportation center twenty miles south of the Confederate capital. The strategic and tactical war of maneuver that had ranged over northern Virginia for more than three years was transformed into a war of trenches and limited objectives. Miles of earthworks scarred the countryside as the Yankee soldiers ground down Lee's great army.

On March 25 the Confederates attempted to break through the Union line and succeeded briefly, but the Northerners counterattacked and unleashed a massive assault against the Petersburg defenders. The breakthrough occurred on April 2, forcing Lee to pull back and causing the evacuation of the Confederate government from Richmond. Lincoln visited Richmond on April 4 and sat at Jefferson Davis's desk in the Confederate White House.

Meanwhile, the Southerners fell back to the west as Lee raced to a junction of the Richmond and Danville Railroad, hoping that he would be able to unite his army with that of Joseph E. Johnston, which was moving up from North Carolina. The commanders hoped to take advantage of the hilly terrain around Danville and stand off the armies of Grant and Sherman. Grant's army, however, moved faster than Lee expected, and the Southerners lost a day waiting for a supply train at

Amelia Court House. In the meantime, Yankee cavalry seized the Richmond and Danville junction, thwarting the Southerners' plans and forcing Lee to move toward Lynchburg as his next best defensible position.

On April 6, about one-quarter of Lee's army was captured at Saylers Creek. When he learned of his losses, the Southern commander altered his line of march and continued to lead his remaining 30,000 men in a north-by-west arch toward Lynchburg. Grant was not far behind, and his cavalry raced ahead and blocked the Confederates' route at Appomattox Court House. When Lee tried to probe the Federal line on the morning of April 9, he found the enemy *en mass* and in far superior numbers. Lee had no other option than to meet with Grant and negotiate the surrender of his army.

The scene at Appomattox Court House on Palm Sunday in 1865 was a bitter and humiliating ending for the once victorious Confederate army. An aide on Lee's staff secured the use of the home of Wilmer McLean for the meeting between the two principals, and in the front parlor in the early afternoon Grant wrote out the terms of surrender and handed them to Lee to read. Lee responded with a letter of acceptance, and the generals exchanged documents. The officers and men of the Army of Northern Virginia were paroled but their weapons and supplies were relinquished as captured property.

Lee's surrender to Grant was the first of five Confederate surrenders, the last occurring on June 23, 1865. The surrender at Appomattox, however, has been viewed traditionally as the end of the war, because it removed the largest viable Southern army from the field and ended the fighting in Virginia. The war was over.

War is cruelty and you cannot refine it . . . when peace does come, you may count on me for anything. Then I will share with you the last cracker.

Union Gen. William Tecumseh Sherman, 1865

The people must be left nothing but their eyes to weep with over the war.

Union Gen. Philip H. Sheridan,
Shenandoah Valley, 1865

I mean to end this business here.

Union Gen. Ulysses S. Grant,
Petersburg, March 1865

They were trying to corner this old army, but like a brave lion brought to bay at last it is determined to resist to the death, and if it die, it must die game.

Confederate Col. Walter Taylor,
Robert E. Lee's staff, Petersburg, 1865

Country be damned. There is no country. There has been no country, General, for a year or more. You are the country to these men. They have fought for you . . . there are still thousands left who will die for you.

Confederate Gen. Henry Wise, to Robert E. Lee prior to the surrender, April 1865

Our people are tired of war, feel themselves whipped, and will not fight. Our country is overrun, its military reserves greatly diminished, while the enemy's military power and resources were never greater, and may be increased to any extent desired.

Confederate Gen. Joseph E. Johnston, April 1865

The breakthrough at Fort Mahone, nicknamed Fort Damnation by Grant's army, in the Confederate works around Petersburg did not come easily, but its fall during the desperate fighting of April 2, 1865, presaged the end of the ten-month siege. The assault began with one of the greatest bombardments of the war, and the clash of men was as fierce as any combat during the conflict. On the morning after the attack, Thomas Roche photographed several casualties of the 53d North Carolina where they lay in the mud-filled trenches, including the image on the facing page. The tragedy of these dead, however, seemed greater because they died for a cause already lost.

Thank God I have lived to see this. It seems to me that I have been dreaming a horrid dream for four years, and now the nightmare is gone.

Abraham Lincoln, April 3, 1865

Don't kneel to me. That is not right. You must kneel to God only, and thank Him for the liberty you will enjoy hereafter.

Abraham Lincoln, to former slaves during his visit to Richmond, April 1865

Viewed across the canal basin of the James River, the Confederate capitol at Richmond stood as a symbol of Southern independence for almost four years. When Grant's army entered the city on April 3, 1865, they found that the Rebel government had fled and that the departing army had torched the riverfront warehouses to prevent their contents from falling into the hands of the enemy. The fire, however, spread quickly, threatening to engulf the entire city in flames. The soldiers in blue earned a measure of respect and gratitude from the remaining citizens when they quashed the inferno.

It is finished! Oh, my beloved division! Thousands of them have gone to their eternal home, having given up their lives for the cause they knew to be just. The others, alas, heartbroken, crushed in spirit, are left to mourn its loss.

Confederate Gen. George E. Pickett, April 8, 1865

My shoes are gone; my clothes are almost gone. I'm weary, I'm sick, I'm hungry. My family have been killed or scattered. And I have suffered all this for my country. I love my country. . . . But if this war is ever over, I'll be damned if I ever love another country!

An anonymous soldier in Longstreet's corps, during the retreat to Appomattox

Then there is nothing left me to do but to go and see General Grant, and I would rather die a thousand deaths. . . . How easy I could be rid of this! All I have to do is ride along the line and all would be over. But it is our duty to live.

Confederate Gen. Robert E. Lee,
Palm Sunday morning, April 9, 1865

The McLean house at Appomattox Court House (facing page) was the site of the meeting between Grant and Lee and the surrender of the Army of Northern Virginia.

General, unless he offers us honorable terms, come back and let us fight it out!

> *Confederate Gen. James Longstreet,*
> *to Lee regarding Grant, April 9, 1865*

We walked in softly and ranged ourselves quietly about the sides of the room, very much as people enter a sick-chamber when they expect to find the patient dangerously ill.

> *Union Gen. Horace Porter, describing the surrender*
> *room at the McLean house, Appomattox Court House,*
> *Virginia, April 9, 1865*

GEN. ROBERT E. LEE: I am glad to see one real American here.
ELY PARKER (Seneca Indian on Grant's staff): We are all Americans.

> *Appomattox, April 9, 1865*

This will live in history.

> *Unknown Union officer after Lee's surrender to Grant,*
> *April 9, 1865*

The war is over. The rebels are our countrymen again.

Union Gen. Ulysses S. Grant, April 9, 1865

The road was packed by standing troops as he approached, the men with hats off, heads and hearts bowed down. As he passed they raised their heads and looked upon him with swimming eyes. Those who could find voice said good-by, those who could not speak, and were near, passed their hands gently over the sides of Traveller.

Confederate Gen. James Longstreet, Appomattox Court House, April 9, 1865

Men, we have fought through the war together; I have done my best for you; my heart is too full to say more . . . goodbye.

Confederate Gen. Robert E. Lee, April 9, 1865

We are lost in a vision of human tragedy. . . . How could we help but falling on our knees, all of us together, and praying God to pity and forgive us all!

Union Gen. Joshua Chamberlain, Appomattox Court House, April 12, 1865

I felt like anything rather than rejoicing at the downfall of a foe who had fought for so long and valiantly and had suffered so much for a cause, though that cause was, I believe, one of the worst for which a people ever fought.

> *Union Gen. Ulysses S. Grant, reflecting on Lee's surrender at Appomattox*

Before us in proud humiliation stood the embodiment of manhood, with eyes looking level into ours, waking memories that bound us together as no other bonds. Was not such manhood to be welcomed back into a union so tested and assured? . . . We cannot look into those brave, bronzed faces and think of hate and personal mean revenge. Whoever had misled these men, we had not. We had led them back home.

> *Union Gen. Joshua Lawrence Chamberlain, at the surrender ceremonies at Appomattox, April 12, 1865*

We must simply begin with, and mould from, disorganized and discordant elements.

> *Abraham Lincoln, shortly after hearing of Lee's surrender*

My God, what misery this dreadful war has produced, and how it comes home to the doors of almost every one!

Union Gen. George Gordon Meade, April 13, 1865

If the one army drank the joy of victory and the other the bitter draught of defeat, it was a joy moderated by the recollection of the cost at which it had been purchased, and a defeat mollified by the consciousness of many triumphs. If the victors could recall a Malvern Hill, an Antietam, a Gettysburg, a Five Forks, the vanquished could recall a Manassas, a Fredericksburg, a Chancellorsville, a Cold Harbor. How terrible had been the struggle!

New York Times *correspondent William Swinton*

7

The Border of Sorrows

Lincoln's Assassination and Beyond

Abraham Lincoln spent most of the last two weeks of the war at Grant's headquarters in City Point, Virginia, pensive that the end seemed near but remained elusive. When Petersburg was abandoned and Richmond evacuated on April 3, the president toured the Confederate capital with a small entourage. He returned to City Point anxious to hear if Lee had surrendered. While letters passed between the two generals, affairs in Washington called for Lincoln's personal attention.

The president returned to Washington on the evening of April 9, and the first telegraph he received was from Grant, announcing that Lee had surrendered that morning at Appomattox Court House. As news of the surrender spread, all of Washington celebrated. Lincoln and his cabinet began to outline the reconstruction of the South. Privately, the president and his wife discussed their future, life after his second term. They discussed trips overseas and a visit to the West before resettling and opening a law office in Springfield or Chicago.

On the morning of April 14 the newspaper announced that the president, the first lady, and General and Mrs. Grant would be attending the play *Our American Cousin* at Ford's Theater that evening. The box office quickly sold out, and scalpers made a significant profit selling 75¢ and $1 tickets for $2.50.

About midday, news of the president's plans reached actor John Wilkes Booth, a Southern sympathizer and a man on a mission. Earlier he had conspired to kidnap the president and deliver him to Richmond to be exchanged for prisoners of war. Now he plotted to kill Lincoln and other high-ranking Federal officials, hoping that Jefferson Davis and any Confederate armies that had not yet surrendered would exploit the situation and still gain Southern independence. Booth would kill Lincoln and co-conspirators George Atzerodt would dispatch Vice President Andrew Johnson and Lewis Paine would remove Secretary of State William H. Seward. The three murders were to be carried out simultaneously at 10:15 P.M.

The Lincolns were late in getting to the theater. The play had already started, but the appearance of the president and his party, which lacked the Grants, prompted spontaneous applause and cheering from the audience. The play resumed, and during the second scene of the third act, the door to the presidential box opened and Booth slipped in. A burst of laughter from the theatergoers was interrupted by a single gunshot. Lincoln slumped forward. Booth also slashed the arm of one of the other box occupants before leaping to the stage. His foot caught on one of the flag decorations, and he crashed to the floor below. As he limped off stage he yelled something, but no one quite understood what he said.

The other conspirators failed in their assignments. Atzerodt made no attempt to approach the vice president; Paine found Seward sick in bed and attacked him but was restrained. By morning, as Lincoln lay dying in a bed in a boardinghouse across from the theater, all those who had conspired with Booth, including his kidnapping plan, had been apprehended. The assassin, however, had escaped to Virginia by way of Maryland. He was found at a farm in northern Virginia on April 26 and shot during the apprehension.

Lincoln died on the morning of April 15, one of the last casualties of the war. His funeral train retraced the route that he had taken in 1861 for his inauguration. The track was lined with thousands of mourners all the way to Springfield, where he was buried.

I restore to its proper place this flag which floated here during peace, before the first act of this cruel rebellion. I thank God I have lived to see this day, and to be here to perform this, perhaps the last act of my life, of duty to my country.

> *Maj. Gen. Robert Anderson, Fort Sumter,*
> *April 14, 1865*

Now, by God, I'll put him through. That is the last speech he will ever make.

> *John Wilkes Booth, April 11, 1865*

Sic Semper Tyrannis! (Thus always to tyrants!)

> *John Wilkes Booth, allegedly after mortally*
> *wounding Abraham Lincoln, Ford's Theater,*
> *Washington, D.C., April 14, 1865*

On the fourth anniversary of the surrender of Fort Sumter, Maj. Gen. Robert Anderson returned to the site of his former command. The day's ceremonies included the raising of the same flag that had flown over the fort in 1861. President Lincoln had been invited, but he chose to stay in Washington and attend a play. The next day, Sumter's flag was lowered to half-staff following news of the president's assassination.

Now he belongs to the ages.

Edwin M. Stanton, secretary of war, at Lincoln's deathbed, April 15, 1865

The South has lost its best friend.

Union Maj. Gen. Joshua Lawrence Chamberlain, on the death of Lincoln, April 15, 1865

From an abolitionist point of view, Mr. Lincoln seemed tardy, cold, dull, and indifferent. But measuring him by the sentiment of his country, he was swift, zealous, radical, and determined.

Frederick Douglass, April 1865

I certainly have no special regard for Mr. Lincoln; but there are a great many men of whose end I would much rather heard than his. I fear it will be disastrous for our people, and I regret it deeply.

Jefferson Davis, April 19, 1865

Lincoln—old Abe Lincoln—killed—murdered. . . . It is simply maddening, all of this. . . . I know this foul murder will bring down worse miseries on us.

Mary Boykin Chesnut, April 22, 1865

What has gone before takes something with it, and when this is of the dear, nothing can fill the place. All the changes touched the border of sorrows.

Major Gen. Joshua Lawrence Chamberlain, 1865

The mass of the people south will never trouble us again. They have suffered terrifically, and I now feel disposed to befriend them.

Union Gen. William Tecumseh Sherman, April 28, 1865

I did all in my power to break up the government, but I have found it a useless undertaking, and am now resolved to stand by the government as earnestly and honestly as I fought it.

Former Confederate Gen. Nathan Bedford Forrest

The climax of the investigation into the assassination of the president was the trial of eight co-conspirators before a military tribunal. All were found guilty. Four (Lewis T. Paine, David Herold, George Atzerodt, and Mary Surratt) were sentenced to death and hanged at the Washington Arsenal (above). Three (Samuel Arnold, Michael O'Laughlin, and Samuel A. Mudd) received life sentences. One (Edward Spangler) was sentenced to six years' imprisonment. A ninth co-conspirator, John Surratt, was extradicted from Egypt in 1866 and acquitted. In 1869 President Andrew Johnson pardoned the surviving prisoners.

Madam, do not train up your children in hostility to the government of the United States. Remember, we are one country now. Dismiss from your mind all sectional feeling, and bring them up to be Americans.

> *Robert E. Lee, during his term as president of*
> *Washington College, Lexington, Virginia, 1867*

Nations, like individuals, are punished for their transgressions. We got our punishment in the most sanguinary and expensive war of modern times.

> *Ulysses S. Grant, 1885*

To celebrate the Union victory, the War Department ordered a grand review in Washington of the main Northern armies (facing page), George Gordon Meade's Army of the Potomac and William Tecumseh Sherman's Army of Georgia and Army of the Tennessee. Meade's 80,000 veterans paraded down Pennsylvania Avenue on May 23, and Sherman's 65,000 men on May 24. "The sight was simply magnificent," recalled Sherman. "The column was compact, and the glittering muskets looked like a solid mass of steel, moving with the regularity of a pendulum."

I believe there is today, because of the war, a broader and deeper patriotism in all Americans; that patriotism throbs the heart and pulses the being as ardently of the South Carolinian as of the Massachusetts Puritan.

James Longstreet, 1895

It was thought to be a great thing to charge a battery of artillery or an earthwork lined with infantry. . . . We were very lavish of blood in those days.

Former Confederate Gen. Daniel Harvey Hill

This war was a fearful lesson, and should teach us the necessity of avoiding wars in the future.

Ulysses S. Grant

[The war] was a remnant of the inherited curse of sin. We had purged it away, with blood offerings.

Joshua Lawrence Chamberlain

The war has made us a nation of great power and intelligence. We have but little to do to preserve peace, happiness and prosperity at home, and the respect of other nations. Our experience ought to teach us the necessity of the first; our power secures the latter.

Ulysses S. Grant

Dear wife, this is not the fate to which I invited you when the future was rose-colored to us both, but I know you will bear it even better than myself, and that of us two, I alone will ever look back reproachfully on my past career.

Jefferson Davis, April 1865

8

A Soldier's Tale

Johnny Reb and Billy Yank

More than three million men (and a few hundred women) bore arms during the conflict of 1861–65. Southerners viewed the struggle as a second American Revolution whose goal was to finish the work of the Founding Fathers. Northerners fought for a vision of democracy. Most of them were idealists willing to pay the ultimate price for liberty. All of them craved adventure, but none of them knew what lay ahead. Both sides viewed the other as cowardly and soulless and likely to flee once a flag was waved or a charge begun. For some the war was a rite of passage, much as it was the nation itself.

Romantic visions of warfare faded quickly in the brutal chaos of actual battle. Many ran, but most of these citizen soldiers lost their fear after a few moments of combat. They sensed a thrill to the fighting and seemed almost oblivious to the deadly projectiles thrown at them, at least until they were struck by one. Here the men paid a high price for the outdated tactics of their commanders, who failed to adapt their strategies to the advances in weaponry.

As deadly as the battlefield was, twice as many soldiers died from disease as from bullets. Most of the men were accustomed to living in the open with few neighbors in sight. Once in the army, thousands of men were massed together in tent cities. Their water was contaminated, their food was inedible, and there was little understanding of the relationship between hygiene and disease. Few recruits had any resistance to community diseases because of their isolated backgrounds, and thus so-called childhood diseases raged epidemically through the camps.

Sadness, anguish, hunger, deprivation, and death generated a bond that united the soldiers in ways that nothing else could. They coped with homesickness and the loss of comrades in many ways.

Some found solace in drinking. Others balanced camp life with gambling and sports, particularly baseball and, during the winter, snowball fights. Some were joined by their families in camp. For others there were camp followers and, near the larger cities, bordellos.

Music played a significant role in the camps. It expressed the feelings of the men and also inspired them on the battlefield. Soldiers who could play instruments were popular, and banjo players and fiddlers were the most popular. At first the camps were filled with jovial tunes and proud ballads, but as the war continued the music changed to songs of loneliness and homesickness, heart-wrenching songs that conveyed the deepest feelings of the men. Sometimes sad songs were banned by unit commanders who feared that morale was too low.

Occasionally, men on both sides sang together while still deployed on the battlefield. Such moments underlined how the men in both armies shared a common heritage. They spoke the same language, worshiped the same God, and held the same values. They swapped newspapers and even letters and bartered tobacco for coffee as often as they could. They were fiercely independent, passionate in their loyalties, and sometimes noble, but above all they were Americans.

The vast majority of soldiers were literate, and so their diaries and letters preserve a sense of what the fighting men of the war thought of their predicament. They spent a great deal of their time writing or dictating letters to their friends and family, maintaining a link with the home they remembered from before the war and the home to which they hoped to return afterward. When they discussed themselves and their ideals, the common soldier spoke of freedom, honor, and liberty as eloquently and fervently as Abraham Lincoln or Jefferson Davis.

The actual soldier, North and South, with all his ways, his incredible dauntlessness, habits, practices, tastes, language, his fierce friendship, his appetite, rankness, his superb strength and animality, lawless gait, and a hundred unnamed lights and shades of the same, will never be written.

Walt Whitman

The strongest ties between human beings are not cemented in safety, luxury, and comfort. It is in the dividing by a hungry soldier, with a hungrier comrade, the last morsel of meat, the binding up of each others' wounds, the lending of courage from one heart to another.

Union Capt. Horace H. Shaw, 1st Maine Infantry

Every one seems to know that his life, liberty, and property are at stake, hence we never can be whipped.

Confederate Lt. Hannibal Paine, Tennessee, 1861

No one loves wife or family more than I. Yet my country has claims upon me strong as that of home or family.

Union Cpl. Lyman G. Bennett, Missouri, 1861

We fight for blessings bought by the blood and treasure of our Fathers. I will fight till I die if necessary for the liberties which you have so long enjoyed.

Union soldier William S. Stewart, in a letter to his parents, Missouri, 1861

I do feel that the liberty of the world is placed in our hands to defend, and if we are overcome then farewell to freedom.

Union Pvt. Josiah Perry, Massachusetts, 1862

I intend to fight them to the last. . . . I will kill them as long as I live even if peace is made I never will get done with them.

Confederate soldier John Collins, Virginia, 1862

Cheerfully I determine never to lay down my rifle as long as a Yankee remains on Southern soil.

Confederate Sgt. Harry Lewis, Mississippi, 1862

What is home with all it endearments, if we have not a country freed from every vestige of the anarchy, and the tyrannical and blood thirsty despotism which threatens on every side to overwhelm us?

Union Pvt. George W. Beidleman, Pennsylvania, 1862

I trust I am prepared to offer myself a bloody sacrifice on the altar of my adopted country, if need be.

Union Pvt. James Carrie, Missouri, February 3, 1862

My dear father, this is my last letter to you. I've been struck by a piece of shell, and my right shoulder is horribly mangled. I know that death is inevitable. I will die far from home, but I have friends here who are kind to me. May we meet again in heaven.

J. R. Montgomery, Spotsylvania Company, Virginia

Dear Surgeon Ebersoll, my limb causes much curiosity among the surgeons here. They say it is the best amputation they ever saw. They wonder how it was ever done, and wish to know how you did the work. Thanks to you for your skill in taking off my limb.

Alexander Ivy, 7th Wisconsin Infantry

There is one thing about which every man who has been in a battle seems to be pretty sure & that is that he doesn't want to go into another if he can avoid it.

Union Col. Robert Gould Shaw, March 28, 1862

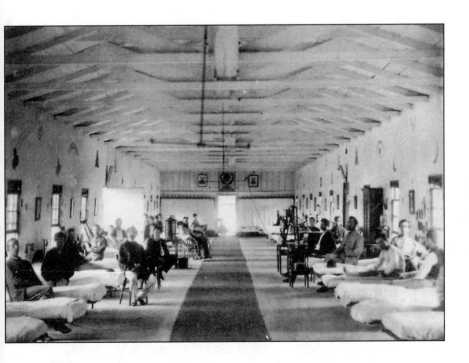

There was an orderly in one of our regiments, and he and the corporal always slept together. Well, the other night, the corporal had a baby, for the corporal turned out to be a woman! She'd been in three or four fights!

Union soldier Solomon Newton,
10th Massachusetts Infantry

Our men must prevail in combat, or lose their property, country, freedom, everything. . . . On the other hand, the enemy, in yielding the contest, may retire into their own country, and possess everything they enjoyed before the war began.

Confederate soldier John B. Jones, Virginia, 1863

Should we the youngest and brightest nation of all the earth bow to traitors and forsake the graves of our Fathers? No, no, never.

Union soldier Joseph Fardell, Illinois, 1863

Oh my country, how my heart bleeds for your welfare. If this poor life of mine could save you, how willingly would I make the sacrifice.

Union Cpl. Joseph H. Griner, Pennsylvania, 1863

My country, glorious country, if we have only made it truly the land of the free. . . . I count not my life dear unto me if only I can help that glorious cause along.

Union soldier Nelson Chaplin, New York, 1863

A man in fighting for liberty . . . can realize that he died to save something better than life.
Union soldier Edgar Ketcham, New York, 1863

Oh God! Thy price for freedom is a DEAR ONE!
Union soldier John Ketcham, New York, 1863

I am engaged in the glorious cause of liberty and justice, fighting for the rights of man—fighting for all that we of the South hold dear.
Confederate Cpl. Phineas M. Savery, Alabama, 1863

Tell mother I died for her and my country.
Confederate soldier Charles T. Haskell Jr., dying words, July 10, 1863

We are not yet ready for peace—and want a good deal of purging still.
Union Col. Robert Gould Shaw, 54th Massachusetts, July 6, 1863

$\mathbf{W}$e should . . . slay them like wheat before the scythe at harvest time. I certainly love to live to kill the usurping vandals. If it is a sin to hate them; then I am guilty of the unpardonable one.

Confederate Sgt. H. Christopher Kendrick,
Georgia, 1863

Emancipation without deportation
Sequestration without Litigation
Condemnation without mitigation
Extermination without procrastination
Confiscation without Botheration
Damnation without reservation
And no hesitation until
there is a Speedy termination
to this Southern Confederation.

Union soldier E. J. Sherlock, August 25, 1863

Tell my father that I died with my face to the enemy.

Confederate Col. Isaac E. Avery, North Carolina,
Gettysburg, July 2, 1863

This is a rich man's war, but the poor man has to do the fighting.

Confederate soldier John W. Reese,
North Carolina, 1863

Sergeant Eagers went down to the slaughter pen one day where he got hold of two hooves of an old cow. We cooked those hooves five times and drank the hot broth, and thought it was a pretty good meal.

Union soldier August Rhymers, 15th Missouri, at Chattanooga

We are fighting for matters real and tangible . . . our property and our homes, they for matters abstract and intangible.

Confederate Pvt. H. C. Munford, Texas, 1864

We are fighting for the Union, a high and noble sentiment. They are fighting for independence and are animated by passion and hatred against invaders. . . . It makes no difference whether the cause is just or not. You can get an amount of enthusiasm that nothing else will excite.

Union soldier Frederick Bartleson, Illinois, 1864

God pity this south land when we are done with it.

Union Pvt. Chauncey Cooke, Wisconsin, May 3, 1864

L̷et [the war] be long . . . if we give it up now we will certainly be the most degraded people on earth.

Confederate Pvt. John Weaton, Mississippi, 1864

Our martyred Saviour was called seditious, and I may be pardoned if I rejoice that I am a rebel.

Confederate Capt. Robert Emory Park, Alabama, 1864

If I do get hurt it will be only for my Country and my Children but for Liberty all over the World that I risked my life, for if Liberty should be crushed here, what hope would there be for the cause of Human Progress anywhere else?

Union Cpl. George H. Codman, Ohio, 1864

A fellow sufferer very truly remarked that we are in a very bad state—the state of Virginia.

Union Pvt. Frank Wilkerson, 1864

Our country is gone, our cause is lost.

Confederate Pvt. Sam Watkins, Tennessee, 1864

Blow, Gabriel, blow! My God, let him blow! I am ready to die!

Unknown Confederate soldier at Appomattox, 1865

War is cruel in all its parts—a horrid blessing sent on mankind in a shape curiously like a curse; and in all wars the purest form of squalid misery to which God's image is anywhere reduced has ever been found in the depots of prisoners.

Union Lt. Col. Charles Francis Adams Jr.,
Massachusetts, January 8, 1865

Future years will never know the seething hell and infernal background of this war. Oh, the sad scenes I witness, scenes of death, anguish, amputations, friendlessness, hungering, and thirsting young hearts.

Walt Whitman

In my latest writing and utterance, I here repeat my unmitigated hatred to . . . the vile Yankee race.

Edmund Ruffin, June 17, 1865,
prior to committing suicide

Are these things real? . . . Did I see those brave and noble countrymen of mine laid low in death and weltering in their blood? Did I see our country laid waste and in ruins? Did I see soldiers marching, the earth trembling and jarring beneath their measured tread? Did I see the ruins of smouldering cities and deserted homes? . . . Surely they are but the vagaries of mine own imagination.

Confederate Pvt. Sam Watkins, 1st Tennessee Infantry

The real war will never get in the books. . . . The actual soldier of 1861–5, North and South, with all his ways, his incredible dauntlessness, habits, practices, tastes, language, his fierce friendship, his appetite, rankness, his superb strength and animality, lawless gait, and a hundred unnamed lights and shades of camp, I say, will never be written.

Walt Whitman, 1865

We have shared the incommunicable experience of war. We have felt, we still feel, the passion of life to its top. In our youths, our hearts were touched by fire. It was given to us to learn at the outset that life is a profound and passionate thing.

Oliver Wendell Holmes Jr.

Were the thing to be done over again, I would do as I then did. Disappointments have not changed my convictions.

Jefferson Davis, in his postwar memoirs

In great deeds something abides. On great fields something stays. Forms change and pass; bodies disappear; but spirits linger. . . . This is the great reward of service, to give life's best for such high stake that it shall be found again unto life eternal.

Joshua Lawrence Chamberlain,
from his postwar writings